Construction Industry Scheme

Guidance and Commentary

2nd edition

Howard Royse

First edition June 2015
This edition November 2017

Construction Industry Scheme

Guidance and Commentary

2nd edition

Howard Royse

Published by:

Claritax Books Ltd
6 Grosvenor Park Road
Chester, CH1 1QQ

www.claritaxbooks.com

ISBN: 978-1-908545-95-4

Other titles from Claritax Books

Other titles from Claritax Books include:

- A-Z of Plant & Machinery
- Capital Allowances
- Discovery Assessments
- Employee Benefits & Expenses
- Employment Status
- Entrepreneurs' Relief
- Financial Planning with Trusts
- Furnished Holiday Lettings
- Main Residence Relief
- Pension Tax Guide
- Research & Development
- Residence: The Definition in Practice
- Stamp Duty Land Tax
- Tax Chamber Hearings
- Tax Losses
- VAT Registration
- Venture Capital Schemes

See www.claritaxbooks.com for details of further titles due for publication in the coming months.

About the author

Howard Royse studied accountancy at the University of East Anglia and qualified as a chartered accountant with a top 20 firm in 1985. He has been in practice as a sole practitioner for more than 20 years and has acted as the financial consultant for several construction companies.

He took up the post as the construction industry representative for the ICAEW in 2004 and engaged in discussions with HMRC for what is now the current CIS, and for the employment status indicator, and he advised HMRC in the restructuring of the CIS repayment system. He has briefed the Public Accounts Committee for meetings with HMRC on CIS and has published several articles in the ICAEW *Taxline*, and in *Taxation* magazine. He is a member of the ICAEW Small Business Tax Committee.

Howard may be contacted at howard.royse@btconnect.com or on 01953 788163.

About the publisher

Claritax Books publishes specialist tax titles, complementing what is on offer from the larger tax publishers. Typically, our books cover niche topics in greater depth or take a more practical approach to particular tax issues. Our titles are written for accountants (both in-house and in practice), tax advisers, employers, lawyers and other professionals. Our authors include barristers, solicitors, accountants and other experienced tax specialists.

Claritax Books titles cover (among other topics) tax appeals, capital allowances, the statutory residence rules, CGT reliefs, the CIS scheme, pensions and trusts, stamp duty land tax, VAT, employment taxes and furnished holiday lettings. Visit www.claritaxbooks.com for details of all our books.

Claritax Books is a trading name of Claritax Books Ltd (company number 07658388, VAT number 114 9371 20). The company is based in Chester, England.

Acknowledgements

The first person I should mention is Richard Shooter, who was the previous ICAEW liaison on CIS. After I had bombarded him with questions on the Scheme, he suggested I should take over and recommended me for the (voluntary) post. He was right, in that the work itself can be rewarding.

At the Institute, Anita Monteith has given me much sound advice and guidance in my dealings with HMRC, as well as elegantly editing some of my more polemic writings.

Finally, my wife Emma has been there to listen whilst I gassed on about tax issues and the structure of the book, and to provide a regular supply from the Nespresso machine.

Postscript

Since the publication of the first edition, Ken Claydon has retired from HMRC. Ken's work on CIS preceded my involvement; he was always prepared to listen to sensible suggestions and to take the necessary steps to make the scheme function more effectively. He set standards that will be very difficult for his successors to match.

Abbreviations

BACS	Bankers' Automated Clearing Services
CGT	Capital Gains Tax
Ch.	Chapter
CIOT	Chartered Institute of Taxation
CIRIP	Construction Industry Review Implementation Panel
CIS	Construction Industry Scheme
CISOF	Construction Industry Scheme Operational Forum
CISR(M)	Construction Industry Scheme Reform Manual
CITB	Construction Industry Training Board
CLA	Customer Level Agents
CSCS	Construction Skills Certification Scheme
CT	Corporation Tax
DMB	Debt and Management Board
EPS	Employer Payment Summary
EWCA	England and Wales Court of Appeal
EWHC	England and Wales High Court
FA	Finance Act
FPS	Full Payment Submission
FTT	First-tier Tribunal
GC(s)	General Commissioner(s)
GPS	Gross Payment Status
HMRC	HM Revenue & Customs
ICAEW	Institute of Chartered Accountants in England and Wales
ICTA	Income and Corporation Taxes Act
NI(C)	National Insurance (Contributions)
OTS	Office of Tax Simplification
PAYE	Pay As You Earn
Pt.	Part
QS	Quantity Surveyor
Reg.	Regulation
RIA	Regulatory Impact Assessment
RTI	Real Time Information
S.	Section
SA	Self Assessment
Sch.	Schedule
SDLT	Stamp Duty Land Tax

SI	Statutory Instrument
SMP	Statutory Maternity Pay
SPP	Statutory Paternity Pay
SSA	Scheme Specific Agents
SSP	Statutory Sick Pay
TTQT	Tax Treatment Qualifying Tests
UKFTT	UK First-tier Tribunal
UTR	Unique Taxpayer Reference
VAT	Value Added Tax

Table of contents

1. History

2. Basics of CIS – April 2007 to date

3. Scope of construction operations

Reading notes

For the purposes of brevity, businesses in construction will be classed as either limited companies or the self-employed. The latter is intended to encompass partnerships and any limited liability partnerships operating in construction. Joint ventures are similarly categorised as the constituent parts of the venturers. Trusts may need to register for CIS but are a very small minority.

The tax authorities will be known as HMRC or the Revenue, which was a term used to describe the Inland Revenue and which continues to be used as an abbreviation for Her Majesty's Revenue and Customs.

The Construction Industry Scheme (though initially termed the Construction Industry Tax Deduction Scheme) will be referred to as such and will at times be abbreviated to CIS, and gross payment status to GPS. Other abbreviations will become clear with the reference notes.

Subcontractors are commonly known in the industry as "subbies". This abbreviation will be used merely for variety.

The great majority of self-employed workers in construction are male. Whilst not wishing to ignore or belittle the existence or skills of any female workers, the masculine use of the third person will be used.

There will be the occasional reference to CSCS cards. The Construction Skills Certification Scheme is a database of people working in construction who have a recognised qualification; the cards are a way for each worker to prove these qualifications. It is very difficult to gain access to a construction site without such a card.

This Scheme is maintained by the CITB. The Construction Industry Training Board seeks to offer and improve construction skills and to encourage employers to offer training. Levies are collected from employers, with the money reinvested as grants to support training initiatives.

Cash flow shortages and difficulty in obtaining payment are common problems in the construction industry, made worse in recent years. They are often cited when problems arise with HMRC. One practical matter to bear in mind is that subcontractors can find themselves in an awkward position; if payment is not forthcoming on an uncompleted contract, simply walking off site in the hope of using that as leverage against the contractor is not an effective approach – typically, the contract terms state that in that event, the subcontractor forfeits any claim to further payment.

Recovering materials is an unlikely option as doing so is likely to involve damaging the work of others and the contract will stipulate penalties thereto.

Though not a direct tax issue, awareness of construction frameworks may be useful. Essentially, these are approved lists of suppliers who will be asked to tender for contracts that form part of a larger works programme. These frameworks are commonly used by public sector bodies as expediencies for the tender process. There has been much debate recently about such frameworks being extended to smaller contracts, to allow smaller businesses to contract directly. Loss of GPS would undoubtedly threaten such a business obtaining or retaining its membership on a framework.

The directorate within HMRC that collects and pursues tax is the Debt and Management Board, or DMB. There will be some references to DMB, who have not been especially helpful to construction businesses. Repayments of CIS on account and by BACS took some time to be approved, and there continue to be denials of offset of repayments due against other liabilities. The appropriate representations have been made.

Introduction

The principal purpose of this book is to act as a practical guide to dealing with the requirements of the Construction Industry Scheme. The HMRC publication CIS340 sets out these requirements, but not always how they should, or could, be best dealt with. This book offers advice in how to proceed and what to avoid, drawn from years of experience from representing clients in the accountancy profession, liaising with HMRC and from working in the construction industry.

It is assumed that the reader will have access to CIS340. This is no longer available in paper format, and with the change to the gov.uk website, the people in HMRC dealing with CIS have had to insist that it is retained in PDF format, to ensure that the principal guidance is held in one central publication. So, while this is still available – indeed, while the scheme itself is still in force – this book acts as a complement to that publication, whilst including some interesting facts that HMRC may not wish to be broadcast.

The legislation governing CIS is at sections 57 to 77 and Schedules 11 to 12 of the *Finance Act* 2004 and in the *Income Tax (Construction Industry Scheme) Regulations* 2005.

All facts are correct as at September 2017. The book includes observations on the CIS consultation held by HMRC from June to September 2014, the summary of responses issued in December 2014, and subsequent developments.

The views expressed are my own. These should not be regarded as ICAEW policy, though they often coincide.

Howard Royse

1.   History

1.1   Why is there a Construction Industry Scheme?

For the majority of the working population of the construction industry, for the accountancy profession and for HMRC, CIS is a given. It has always been there. But why? How come one industry has been singled out such that most individual self-employed workers and a lot of businesses are told, "you cannot be trusted to pay your tax"?

Arguably, that is no different to every employee. Under Pay As You Earn, income tax and National Insurance is deducted at source and what employees receive net, is theirs to spend – unless the tax codes are wrong, or something changes in the tax year. However, most employees do not complete a tax return and would choose not to. Even HMRC regard that as unnecessary form-filling. So, PAYE is accepted as an efficient way of collecting tax.

But businesses are different. They have expenses to pay, their profit – taxable or reported – is less clear-cut than a salary, and they don't always know if they are going to be paid. And that has always been true for those in construction, especially in the last few years where subcontractors have been used as a source of finance when the banks decided to raise the financial drawbridge.

With rare exceptions, companies and self-employed individuals receive payment in full, whether it is by raising invoices or cash/card on delivery. So why is the construction industry treated so differently?

1.2   The underlying logic

To understand the motivation of the Revenue to apply additional regulations to one particular industry, we need to go back to the early 1970s.

Stories of industrial action, flying pickets and "scab" labour were front page news every week of the year. The construction industry was as affected by this as any other industry. For three months in 1972, a strike was organised by building labourers with a view to obtaining a minimum wage and improved working conditions.

Tension had been on the increase for many years due to building companies using self-employed workers who were content to be paid cash in hand and accepted the risks of unsafe conditions and equipment. Taxes and time-consuming paperwork were saved and arguably savings were passed on to the end client.

"Lump labour" or more commonly "the lump" were terms used to describe this itinerant and mostly non-unionised workforce. On site, injuries were commonplace. Almost daily a death would occur on a site somewhere and complaints were not encouraged.

Some workers chose not to be employed, which suited the contractors as there was a demand for those who were less particular about their working conditions. The workers would class themselves as subcontractors, leaving the engaging companies with handfuls of handwritten invoices from a large number of "John Smiths". Each John Smith was, therefore, responsible for declaring his income to the Revenue. However questionable the status of each person's self-employment, for the most part, the engagers were free from any responsibility.

1.3 The Revenue's response

The original scheme of certification and flat rate deduction at source on the labour element of payments was introduced in FA 1971 and came into effect in the following year. However, the certificates were easily transferable. This was addressed in F(No 2)A 1975 (the second *Finance Act* of 1975) with the aim of making the identification of subcontractors more certain than before.

1.4 The Construction Industry Scheme 1975-1999

The *Income Tax (Subcontractors in the Construction Industry) Regulations* 1975 were introduced to turn the engaging contractors effectively into the Revenue's policemen. The framework established is largely the same as is in place today, being:

- whether the activity comes within the scope of CIS;
- the identification of the subcontractor;
- establishing whether the subcontractor should be paid gross or net;
- the granting, retention and loss of gross payment status;

- proof of deduction and reporting to the Revenue by the contractor;
- payment of those deductions to the Revenue by the contractor;
- redemption of the deductions by the subcontractor against tax.

The activities covered by the scheme were defined; these included the erection and demolition of buildings, their alteration and repair – as well as a host of ancillary services such as plastering and painting, installation of heating, lighting, drains and windows. The scheme has always applied to construction operations in the UK only.

The regulations applied to businesses recognisably involved in the construction industry, local authorities, development corporations, housing associations and subcontractors providing labour for those bodies. It also included businesses which spent more than a certain amount on construction operations. This annual expenditure limit is currently, as it has been for several years, £1 million.

The annual amount was intended to exclude the majority of non-industry businesses and all private individuals from being involved in paperwork in relation to small building projects. In recent years, HMRC have been at pains to point out that buy-to-let landlords are not intended to be included, unless that is the main activity or source of income of an individual.

The main point of the scheme was to identify contractors and subcontractors and to regulate payments from one to another. A subcontractor may be only one person, up to a large organisation providing construction services – such that the main contractor may not undertake any work at all, merely commissioning and being the project manager. Therefore, a business may be a contractor and subcontract itself to another contractor.

Two classes of subcontractor were recognised by the scheme. Those who were already registered with the Revenue as being involved in the industry and whose tax record showed a good record of compliance could apply for an exemption certificate, known as a 714. This entitled the subcontractor to be paid gross, in exchange for a tax voucher, a 715. The subcontractor, as with other trades, prepared accounts, submitted a tax return and settled the tax liability. As long as the good compliance record was maintained, the certificate would be renewed every three years.

The engaging contractor would retain the vouchers as proof of the certification and exemption of the need to make deductions.

All other subcontractors suffered a flat rate deduction at source on the labour elements of their contracts – not on any materials provided or plant hire costs incurred. This part of the scheme was known as SC60. The contractor kept a separate card for each subcontractor and paid these deductions to the Revenue monthly, alongside the PAYE liability. An annual return CIS36, much like the P35, had to be made at the same time as the normal PAYE returns.

The subcontractor received a certificate SC60, typically monthly, as proof of tax deducted. Accounts needed to be prepared and the tax liability calculated in exactly the same way as for the certificated worker or business. The certificates would be compiled by tax year, not accounting year, and redeemed against tax and Class 4 NI, leaving a net payment or repayment due. In those days of exclusively paper returns, the original certificates had to be sent to the Revenue by the subcontractor as proof of deductions and to prevent duplicate claims.

From the Revenue's point of view, this made collection more certain and much quicker. The burden fell mostly on the contractors for whom little sympathy was felt given the extent of complicity in maintaining the lump. If any of the subcontractors continued not to declare their earnings, the deduction ensured that most of the tax due was collected.

For the tax-compliant subcontractors who became part of the scheme, there was the option of being paid gross. For the others, although their net pay might be lower, at least their tax liability was being saved for them by the deductions. Given the relative rate of deduction – 30% at the beginning – this became a savings scheme, used to pay for Christmas or the family holiday. This thought process remains with us and explains why many businesses prefer to remain net paid.

Those subbies who could not live with the scheme moved into the domestic market, and the "how-much-for-cash" mentality continues to be a significant part of the UK's black economy.

With a few changes to regulation and rates of deduction, this is how the scheme operated for the next 24 years. There was an element of guilt within the industry arising from the lump, a lot of payments were still being made in cash, so CIS was accepted. Receiving and retaining gross payment status was not too difficult, you had to have a bad record of compliance to fail the Revenue's tests. For those that did, there was an underground market trading in 714s.

The Revenue decided that they had been too lenient in granting GPS, also that contractors were not always rigorous in enforcing deductions or enquiring whether the subbie had – or still had – a current 714.

1.5 The Construction Industry Scheme 1999-2007

1.5.1 New CIS

Backed up by a huge publicity campaign, the Revenue launched the new CIS in August 1999 to a less than enthusiastic industry. In the first half of the year local offices held meetings, issued guidance documents and tried hard to explain the steps required. Justification of the changes was less well articulated.

The legal framework was set out in sections 559 to 567 ICTA 1988 and in s. 53 of FA 1999.

The launch date of 1 August 1999 arrived with neither industry nor the Revenue thoroughly prepared. The new scheme itself confused many, applications for new certificates and vouchers were left late and created a backlog, transitional arrangements were unclear and the provision of a sufficient number of accurate vouchers at the right time proved beyond the capability of the Revenue.

Beforehand, your business had a 714 or it didn't. Now a new system of certificates, vouchers and regulations came into force.

Everyone working in the industry had to be registered. All businesses needed one of three levels of Revenue verification.

The minimum requirement for a subcontractor was a CIS4 – a registration card. These could be obtained from a local tax office on production of proof of identity and an NI number. The card contained basic information including the UTR. The effect of ownership of such a card is discussed in **Chapter 13** (self-employment and its interaction with CIS).

Most of these were CIS4P (for Permanent), unless a CIS4T was issued – T for Temporary, with a given expiry date. Payment to a subcontractor with an expired card or no card at all was a breach of the rules of the scheme and could affect the GPS of the contractor.

For the holders of these cards, the old SC60 rules continued to apply – tax deduction for the labour element of any charges.

For the old 714 holders, life became rather more complicated.

1.5.2   Certificates

Conditions were imposed for gross payment status, which have remained in place ever since.

The Revenue were looking to restrict the granting of GPS and the rules for qualification were tightened significantly.

1.5.3   The business test

There needs to be a "proper" construction business established in the UK. If the activities of a business include construction operations, the business must be able to demonstrate that it is properly run through a bank account, with a business address and that records are maintained.

Not a difficult hurdle to overcome but the next tests were a lot more stringent.

1.5.4   The turnover test

Businesses, from 1 August 1999, needed to demonstrate that the annual average turnover in three years within the four years to the date of application had exceeded £30,000, excluding materials.

This applied to sole traders, to partnerships at the rate of £30,000 per partner, and to companies at the rate of £30,000 per director (or per shareholder if the company was close). The turnover rules were met only by that generated from construction work.

Given that the £30,000 limit still applies in 2015, it can be appreciated how much of a step this was at the time.

This excluded from GPS many labour-only subcontractors as well as those providing and operating plant. The Revenue identified this end of the payment chain as being that most at risk from non-declaration of tax and set the bar accordingly.

There were some concessions; new businesses could obtain GPS with a turnover of £21,000 in a six month period, to be reviewed after one year. For partnerships and companies, a threshold was set of £200,000 on average over three years irrespective of the number of partners/directors/shareholders, though with a minimum of £140,000 in any one year.

This made starting a new construction business in late 1999 very difficult, given the cash flow implications of 60 days' credit, with that payment being net of tax and retention. It goes some way to explaining the current shortage of trained UK workers (for lack of opportunity) and the influx of skilled workers from overseas.

The coverage of the scheme was not widened or changed in principle. There was some preliminary discussion of reviewing employment status, but this was set aside for the future.

1.5.5   The compliance test

As before, the business needed to have a sound record of compliance, in respect of PAYE, NI, CIS payments and returns, and the other relevant taxes and returns. There was still no mention of VAT, as Revenue and Customs were not merged until 2005. Some leeway was allowed, but not much – the definition of "minor and technical" was introduced.

1.5.6   Classes of certificate

If a business was granted or already held GPS, the standard certificate was the CIS6. As with the CIS4, this was roughly the size of a credit card and included the person's name, a photograph and specimen signature, the name of the business, the UTR and the expiry date. See **Chapter 5** on verification for the problems caused by this card.

The alternative was a CIS5, granted automatically to publicly quoted companies and their subsidiaries, and to businesses with an annual turnover of more than £5 million. Smaller companies could apply for the CIS5 by making a business case in that it was required to secure work with certain contractors, or that a representative of the business would need to spend more than 100 hours per year visiting client head offices.

It does make you wonder who in the Revenue thought it was acceptable for someone in business to waste the best part of three working weeks per year on one element of tax compliance.

1.5.7   Vouchers

The SC60 was replaced with the CIS25 voucher. This was a three part form, completed by the contractor from the details on the subbie's CIS4 and the payment details. One was given to the subbie as a record of deduction and later submission to the Revenue, the second was for retention by the contractor and the third was sent to the Revenue's CIS Processing Centre. This latter form, with all the others in any given month, should have tallied with the monthly CIS payment made. The totals of the deduction details for the tax year for each subcontractor were entered on the annual CIS36 return, submitted with the P35.

Those subcontractors with GPS requested their own vouchers from the Revenue and were responsible for their completion. CIS6 holders completed the three part CIS24, with payment details and the contractor's UTR, retaining one copy and giving the other two to the contractor who kept one and was responsible for the other being submitted to the Revenue. Such gross payments also needed to be detailed, by the total for the tax year for each subcontractor, on the annual CIS36 return.

The process for CIS5 holders was to complete the two-part CIS 23 voucher, giving one to the contractor and sending the other to the Revenue's Processing Centre. It was never made clear why the CIS5 holder did not need its own copy. However, as no construction plc has ever lost its GPS, it did not become an issue.

1.5.8   Gross payment status

The rules were more stringent, and have largely remained so ever since. These are covered in **Chapter 7**.

1.5.9   *Problems with the 1999-2007 scheme*

The Revenue were quite pleased with the initial outcome; the Finance Bill 2004 *Explanatory Notes* stated that the new scheme had identified more than 70,000 subcontractors who were previously unknown.

Larger businesses had sufficient administrative resources to cope with the new rules, but the smaller businesses had trouble understanding and coping with them. As well as running the business, there were the vouchers and tax deductions to deal with – add to that, the time taken presenting the certificate and that is a lot of time for no income.

The vouchers caused the most problems. They were more like banknotes and were expensive to produce. They were often issued with incorrect references. Some subcontractors were told by HMRC that they could only have ten at a time. Others were refused vouchers on the grounds that those previously issued had not been used – they had been but were either still with the contractor or held up at the Processing Centre.

The rate of deduction of tax was reduced in April 2000 to 18% from 23%. This was something of a reaction, and an attempt to match the deductions more closely to the tax due after deduction of expenses and personal allowances.

The protests from business owners that were wasting time driving around the country were listened to and resulted in the reduction of the CIS5 qualifying limit in 2000 to £3 million, and later to £1 million.

There was another amendment in the rules, for those contractors that could not obtain GPS or chose to work without it; in April 2002, for limited companies, CIS deductions suffered could be offset against PAYE/NI/CIS liabilities due – a more immediate cash flow relief than having to wait up to 21 months to offset the corporation tax liability, if indeed there was one.

1.6   Need for change

Problems with vouchers and certificates meant that as early as 2002, the need to change the workings of the scheme was recognised. It was also realised that the inherent design faults were the result of leaving the task solely to Revenue staff. There had been meetings with industry representatives, but insufficient notice had been taken of problems raised.

A consultation document was issued in November 2002 following the Regulatory Impact Assessment of the previous April.

Reform of CIS was announced in the 2003 Budget.

A panel was formed, the Construction Industry Review Advisory – later, Implementation – Panel (CIRIP), on which one side were Revenue staff, on the other representatives from industry bodies, subsequently expanded to include accountancy bodies and payroll professionals and the representatives of a deemed contractors' panel (which had each met with the Revenue separately).

Basic ideas for the new scheme were presented to the Panel; the realities of operating the current and proposed schemes were discussed, and actually listened to – at times.

It was also realised that a scheme based entirely around paper evidence was behind the times. The option of making verifications and submissions online needed to be built in to the system.

Discussions in the House of Commons expressed a general level of disapproval at the level of self-employment in the construction industry, so the new scheme also had to incorporate a greater level of awareness of terms of engagement. The combination of scrapping CIS4 cards, the new Employment Status Indicator, the regular verification of subcontractors and the monthly declaration of their status were all aimed at reducing the levels of self-employment. Early publicity material (for the April 2006 launch) referred to the responsibility of all contractors, and a "fair tax system" and a "level playing field" for the construction industry. Regrettably, the issue of this material was based on an old database, with notification being sent out to defunct firms and deceased subcontractors.

Originally, the new scheme was aimed for launch on 5 April 2005. More time was needed to design and incorporate the e-channel, as well as to consult with software providers. There were still questions over the robustness of the flow of information and fears of a repeated lack of consultation – so, in December 2003, the launch was delayed for a year.

Even so, the Revenue were warned in early 2005 that the proposed April 2006 launch was unachievable, if problems such as had occurred with the online PAYE and Tax Credits were to be avoided. Software developers needed a minimum of 18 months to prepare and still had not been given the specifications.

In the autumn of 2005, many of the Revenue staff were still insistent that everything would be in place, but just as many on the "industry" side disagreed, some withdrawing from CIRIP in protest.

The Revenue chair of the Panel changed around this time, and the new person recognised very quickly that too much was being left to chance. There had been too many problems with other Revenue online channels and answers to questions about the new scheme suggested that the same thing would happen with CIS. In October 2005, it was announced that the launch was to be delayed for another year, to 5 April 2007.

A lot more effort was put into publicity in the lead-up to the new launch date. "Outreach events" were hosted by the industry representatives and the Revenue issued 280,000 contractor packs, to every construction contractor for whom they had details.

Prior to the launch date, the Revenue approved more than 70 different CIS software packages. It was unclear what the take-up of online submission of monthly returns would be – earlier soundings suggested about 25% – so all contractors were sent pre-populated paper returns for the period to 5 May 2007, to be de-activated once a return had been made online.

1.7   April 2007 onwards – the start of the new scheme

The additional year had been necessary and had been used wisely. There were no significant problems from the beginning, bar some difficulties in registration. Sufficient manpower had been given to the CIS telephone helplines to cope with demand.

Online verifications in the first month were 23% of the total, and 19% for the monthly returns. This level rose to one in three then stabilised to March 2008, mostly using the Revenue's own software.

A snapshot of the statistics to April 2008 may be useful at this stage, to demonstrate how the new scheme progressed in its first year, but also to see the level of activity of what was the peak level of business of the industry, prior to the downturn.

There were 176,000 active contractors and about another 100,000 inactive registrations. 90% of contractors engaged fewer than 10 subcontractors. 85% of returns were submitted by the due date. In the six months from October 2007 to March 2008, after the initial amnesty period, 570,000 penalty notices had been issued.

Two in three verifications were made by telephone. Unmatched verifications were about 10%, but only about 1.5% of deductions were made at the higher rate of 30%.

The rate of failure of the TTQT (Tax Treatment Qualifying Tests) compliance tests was 28%. Around half of the appeals were allowed, giving a GPS withdrawal rate of 14%.

In the eight years of its operation, the scheme in its current form has remained largely unchanged. The revision of penalties has been the most significant legislative change; there are a few more changes arising from the 2014 consultation.

Since the first edition of this book was published, there has been an increase in construction activity – the annual yield from CIS now exceeds £5 billion. Pay rates have improved, and though more workers have been paid through CIS (over a million in 2016-17), this does not necessarily mean that they are all full-timers.

It is yet to be established how significant has been the move away from self-employment brought about by the Onshore Intermediaries legislation. A major reduction in tax collected through CIS will raise questions as to its future.

2.   Basics of CIS – April 2007 to date

2.1   Registration

2.1.1   *All businesses*

Any business, from a self-employed individual to a blue-chip publicly quoted company, that is engaged in construction operations must register with HMRC.

Even the largest business must register, as if it is to be paid by another business engaged in construction operations, such as a deemed contractor, then that other business must verify the first business to confirm its registration and to find out the rate of tax deduction that applies.

Registration can be made by telephone to the CIS Contact Centre or by completing and submitting one of forms CIS 301-305.

2.1.2   *Registration forms*

Form CIS301 is for sole traders, paid net of tax; CIS302 is for sole traders applying to be paid gross.

Information required for individuals in CIS301 is the name, address, UTR and NI number; also the date of commencement of trade in construction and the type of work done. It is also an opportunity to advise HMRC of your agent's authorisation for CIS.

For CIS302, the three tests of business, turnover and compliance will be applied. Details of turnover and the business bank account will be requested. The form is screen-based, but needs to be printed and signed, then submitted to the HMRC office at Longbenton. This is the opportunity to add evidence in support of the GPS application such as accounts and copies of invoices received in the name of the applying business. There is no online facility for application for gross payment status.

Form CIS304 is for partnerships. As with sole traders, information needed is the UTR number and address, and the same details for the individual partners, including NI numbers. One partner needs to be nominated as the registering partner, being the one signing the application. The same form is used whether gross payment status or net paid status is being sought; therefore the GPS tests will need details and evidence as with sole traders above.

Form CIS305 is for companies. Information required is the name, address, UTR number and company registration number, and UTR/NI details for each director and company secretary if GPS is sought. Again, the same form is used for GPS or net paid applications and the same evidence will be needed as above.

Trusts can also apply, using the partnership form CIS304, with the UTR for the trust and trustee applying. Joint ventures are dealt with in the same way as partnerships. Non-resident subcontractors, if wishing to avoid the higher rate of deduction, will need to obtain a UTR before completing the appropriate form.

All necessary details should be obtained before seeking CIS registration. The CIS Contact Centre cannot register businesses for self-assessment or corporation tax. There are also online methods of registration as the equivalent of the paper forms.

2.1.3 HMRC's registration process

HMRC's guidance is for businesses to be registered for CIS, assuming all necessary information has been provided, within five working days. The need to prevent delays and unnecessary deductions at the higher rate is recognised.

The address given by the registering business is that to which HMRC will send correspondence regarding CIS. This should be from wherever the business is administered and not a temporary site address.

2.1.4 Registration of multiple schemes

Contractors can elect to establish more than one scheme under the same reference, if preferred for administrative reasons. This application has to be made in writing to HMRC, before the beginning of the tax year in which those multiple schemes will be run.

Law: SI 2005/2045, reg. 3

2.1.5 Change in registration

If a business is taken over during a tax year and the established scheme is to be retained alongside another, this can be done but

14

HMRC require notification within 90 days of the change in ownership.

2.1.6   *Penalties for false registration*

As part of the drive against tax loss from fraud in construction, HMRC have recently introduced new penalties for the provision of false information, which apply to subcontractors as well as contractors.

In their guidance CC/FS41, the overall penalty provision of £3,000 (that applies across the scheme for wrongdoings by contractors) has been extended to cover any reckless or knowingly false provision of information, in the registration process. Lower levels of penalty of £2,000 and £1,000 will apply to less serious transgressions discovered by HMRC. The penalties apply to false information in respect of identity of the applicants, the business and its turnover.

These penalties are not restricted to GPS applicants – they can also be levied on net-paid subcontractors.

2.2   Registration as contractor

This needs to be made separately from basic CIS registration. Again, it is the CIS Contact Centre that needs to be approached in the first place, but the process is handled by the Employers Business Service.

The details mentioned above will be required, together with the PAYE reference and the PAYE Accounts Office reference. However, it is possible for a business to register as a CIS only contractor – this is known as an XP registration.

There is no separate CIS registration number. Contractors are identified through their PAYE reference; for XP contractors, a PAYE reference is allocated.

Details of how to qualify for and obtain gross payment status are set out in **Chapter 7**.

2.3   Payments and tax deductions

2.3.1   *General principles*

A contractor should verify an engaged subcontractor – ideally upon agreement of the contract for services, preferably before work is started and certainly before any payment is made. Guidance on verifications is given in **Chapter 5**.

Once the rate of deduction of tax is established – 0, 20 or 30% – then the payment can be made.

Payment includes anything made by cash, cheque, bank transfer or credit. A payment on account to a subcontractor, even if a round sum on account, falls within CIS reporting requirements.

For all subcontractors whether paid gross or net, it is the sum actually paid with which CIS is concerned. It is the sum paid net of any retention and any deductions for CITB levies, but before VAT that goes onto the monthly return, being the only sum entered for subcontractors with GPS.

2.3.2   *Format of deduction statement*

For those subcontractors who are paid after deduction of tax, the following example of a remittance advice (which the contractor may provide as a substitute for a deduction statement) may be of use:

Example

A Contractor Ltd

PAYE reference 567/YZ89012

Payment on 5 June 2017

Paid to B Subcontractor Ltd   UTR 32109 87654

Work on the CDE project, Westhampton

Gross payment:	Labour	£20,000
	Materials	£15,000
Retention @ 5%		£ (1,750)
Subtotal		£33,250
VAT @ 20%		£ 6,650
CIS tax deducted		£ (3,800)
Payment to account 88-77-66 55443322		**£36,100**

The CIS tax deducted at the standard rate of 20% is calculated on the labour element of the payment, after deduction of the 5% retention withheld by the contractor. 20% of £20,000 less the 5% retention gives £3,800.

Payment is calculated on the value paid to the subcontractor. An application for payment or an invoice may be issued to the contractor, but it is the sum authorised for payment which counts for CIS. The only exception to this is a deduction made from the subcontractor in respect of a CITB levy. There was some confusion at HMRC over this in March 2014, but this has now been resolved and is definitely a pre-CIS deduction.

2.3.3   Indirect payments

If a payment is reduced on account of a contra, i.e. netting off sales and purchase ledger balances, then it is still the gross sum due to the subcontractor that falls within CIS, not the net.

The factoring of debts by the subcontractor makes no difference to CIS. Irrespective of to whom the payment is made, the same rules on deduction, reporting and the issue of statements apply, and apply only to the subcontractor. The position of the factoring agent is the same as that of the subcontractor's bank.

Similarly, payments made by a contractor on behalf of a subcontractor, such as accommodation costs charged to the contractor's account, count as part of the overall payment and should be included in any calculation of tax deduction.

2.3.4   Retentions

Payment of retentions held by the contractor is meant to happen within twelve months of completion of the subcontractor's work; the idea is that the sum is retained should any problems arise that the subcontractor needs to fix, known as "snagging". Quite often, these sums are retained by the contractor for rather longer.

It may be that the contractor needs to re-verify the subcontractor before finally making that payment retention, as the rules that applied at the time of the original project need not apply later. CIS does not recognise projects or retentions, simply payments. The status of the subcontractor could change during the period that the retention money is held and failure to check is unlikely to constitute a reasonable excuse.

2.4   Monthly return

2.4.1   *Methods of submission*

The option of making submissions by paper return ceased in April 2016, so the only acceptable method is online through HMRC's own software or a third party provider. Submissions through EDS are also possible.

2.4.2   *Initiation*

HMRC's system is run through the Government Gateway. The initial registration can be made online, but the scheme needs an activation code which is sent in the post. As this can take several days, and as there can be problems with the acceptance of the code, it is recommended that this process is begun as soon as possible before any subcontractors are paid.

2.4.3   *First return*

The initial online return will have details entered for verified subcontractors. Tax months run from the 6th day of the month that precedes the first payment made to any subcontractors, to the 5th day of the month thereafter. For payments made to subcontractors, the details required in each case are the subcontractor name, UTR, the gross payment made, and in the case of subcontractors paid net of tax, any deduction made from the gross payment for materials and the tax deducted from the payment. There is no recognition in CIS for VAT.

Example – continued

Using the above example, the figures to be declared by A Contractor Ltd in respect of B Subcontractor Ltd, are the gross sum (£33,250), the materials (£14,250, being £15,000 net of 5% retention) and the tax deducted, £3,800.

Payments to contractors at the higher rate of deduction of 30% also need to declare the verification reference.

If more than one payment has been made to a subcontractor in the tax month, the details need to be aggregated; submissions in the return should not be made for individual payments unless there has only been one payment.

2.4.4   Submission to HMRC

The monthly return needs to be submitted to be with HMRC within 14 days, i.e. by the 19th of the month following the 5th.

2.4.5   Nil returns

Nil returns need to be submitted if no payments to subcontractors have been made in the tax month. These can be made by telephone, if the caller is authorised and has the necessary tax references. There is a box on page 4 of the return to indicate that no payments have been made to subcontractors in that month. Pre-populated details should not be deleted in any way.

Exemption from submission can be obtained from HMRC for a six-month period if it is anticipated that no payments to subcontractors will be made during that time, known as a period of inactivity. This can be made by telephone, or by marking the box on page 4 of the return immediately prior to the six-month inactive period. If a payment to a subcontractor is made during that period, even a round sum payment on account, then the return must be made as appropriate and the exemption ends until another inactivity application is made. The inactive period can be extended by calling HMRC before it ends – a new six-month period will commence from that date, though the question will be asked whether the scheme needs to be closed.

This is especially important for contractors releasing retentions to subcontractors. These count as payments to subcontractors, irrespective of how they have been derived.

2.4.6   Paper returns

Up to April 2016, when online filing became mandatory, it was sensible for those contractors with an unreliable broadband service to have a paper return in stock as a fallback. This demonstrated a will to be CIS compliant. Copies of earlier blank forms, completed for the necessary details, had to be accepted by HMRC as proven in the *Scotts Glass* case.

If an online submission cannot be made in time, then sending in either an old blank form or putting the details in a letter is a good idea, backed up with a call to the CIS helpline. Record the date and time of that call. Further details are given in **Chapter 9** on penalties.

Case: *Scotts Glass & Glazing Services v HMRC* [2011] UKFTT 508 (TC)

2.4.7   Other issues regarding returns

If a business is classed as a deemed contractor for part of its business, only payments to subcontractors for operations that fall within CIS need to be reported.

Payments to local authorities or public bodies should be excluded from returns.

A monthly return can be submitted before the 5th of the month, if holidays prevent it from being submitted after then. Returns can be submitted for three future months, if the payments are known or if this is a preferred method of making nil returns.

If an error is identified on a return after it has been submitted online, then the corrected return needs to be re-submitted. This will override the earlier return on the HMRC records. HMRC's preferred method is that errors are reported through the CIS helpline. If that call is made, the copy of the return held by the contractor needs to be amended. Only the CIS helpline can deal with such calls.

If the return is processed but contains an obvious error (such as an extraordinarily high payment to a subcontractor), HMRC will telephone the contractor to resolve the matter. As this is the easiest way of dealing with such problems, it is recommended that contact details are kept up to date with HMRC.

A contractor may elect to make payments quarterly, if the average monthly amount of CIS and PAYE payments will be less than £1,500. Note that this includes National Insurance and student loan payments, but is net of CIS deductions suffered in the case of limited company contractors. Also note that monthly CIS returns must still be submitted.

Law: SI 2005/2045, reg. 4, 8, 39-46

2.5   Payments to HMRC

2.5.1   *Dates and methods*

Sums deducted from subcontractors are paid in conjunction with PAYE. These need to be with HMRC by the 19th of the month following the 5th if paid by cheque or by cash at a post office, or by the 22nd if an online payment is made.

Law: SI 2005/2045, reg. 7, 58

2.5.2   *Interaction with RTI*

When a contractor pays CIS tax deducted to HMRC, these deductions are incorporated with sums due for payment under PAYE and made as one payment.

In order for HMRC to reconcile this payment, this will be compared with the Full Payment Submission (FPS) made under RTI for the PAYE part, and the CIS 300 for CIS deductions. There is no reference to CIS on the FPS.

For a limited company subcontractor that suffers CIS deductions, these are reported to HMRC via RTI on the Employer Payment Summary (EPS). The net payment can be reconciled by HMRC using the FPS, EPS and CIS300. There is no requirement to submit a nil EPS should no CIS deductions be suffered in a month.

This is not available to sole trader and partnership subcontractors, who will report their own PAYE by use of the FPS and may not make any mention of CIS on any EPS that needs to be submitted, but must instead offset the CIS deductions against their self assessment liabilities.

2.6   Deduction statements

2.6.1   *Requirements*

Throughout its history, CIS has demanded that contractors should give subcontractors proof of any tax deducted when payments have been made.

The vouchers of the 1999-2007 scheme were not popular and not easy or economic for HMRC to produce and supply. For the current scheme, no format template was specified by HMRC, almost as a converse reaction.

Instead, a list of requirements was given that needed to be shown on each statement, which are:

- the contractor's name and PAYE reference;
- the end date of the tax month to which the deduction refers;
- the subcontractor's name and UTR;
- the gross amount of the payment;
- the amount of materials deducted from the gross payment in arriving at the tax deducted; and
- the tax deducted.

The example in **2.3.2** above is a typical logical format to include these requirements.

The statement should also include the verification number (with the A suffix) when the 30% higher rate of deduction has been applied.

2.6.2   Rules for deduction statements

It is not necessary for a statement to be issued for each payment made by the contractor to the subcontractor, if more than one payment has been made within a tax month; these can be grouped together, which is particularly useful for any weekly payments that apply. If producing weekly deduction statements is more expedient, that is not a problem for CIS though it increases the likelihood of the subcontractor losing them. Duplicates can be issued, but should be marked as such.

Any payment made, even if all for materials, or as a payment on account or the release of a retention, triggers the need for a statement to be produced and issued. This should be issued to the subcontractor by the 19th of the month following the tax month's end.

The statement has to be in writing or in a format from which the subcontractor can produce a hard copy. This is in case it needs to be presented to HMRC.

The sums shown on the deduction statements must reconcile with the figures disclosed on the monthly returns. A discrepancy may cause problems for the subcontractor when the CIS deductions are redeemed and HMRC cannot reconcile the records – deductions are redeemed by tax year and not the subcontractor's accounting period (unless they are the same). This may lead to an inspection of the contractor's records.

3. Scope of construction operations

3.1 Introduction

This is not an area that is discussed regularly in meetings with HMRC, or that has been the subject of much contention. This is because HMRC officers have little practical experience of the construction industry and many accountants only understand part of what their clients have told them.

There are meetings with trade bodies but unless there is a new process, this rarely comes up.

3.2 Basics

The main focus of operations that are included in CIS are "construction, alteration, repair, extension, demolition or dismantling of buildings or structures (whether permanent or not), including offshore installations."

The principles are set out in s. 74 of FA 2004 and cover most operations. A useful list of operations can be found in HMRC's *Construction Industry Scheme Reform Manual* at CISR 14330, which is indexed to guidance as to whether each operation falls within or is out of CIS.

This is only guidance and not law. It may be that one operation is not included or has not been correctly interpreted. However, the guidance has been subject to over 40 years of fine-tuning so any omissions are likely to be with new processes. If something is not covered, the safest policy is probably to assume that it is within CIS.

Some principles will override others. For example, solar panels on the roof of a new building; s. 74(2)(c) mentions the "installation in any building ... of heating, lighting ... power supply", but a solar panel is *on* the building and has been manufactured elsewhere. Here, the guidance says that such installations are within CIS, presumably on the basis that all heating and lighting equipment is understood to be part of the building – even though the capture of solar power may be complementary to another source.

Law: FA 2004, s. 74
Guidance: CISR 14330

3.3   Inclusion

One general principle is that if the activity of a subcontractor is partly within CIS, then the whole of the work undertaken within a given project is within CIS. For example, if a subcontractor is fitting floor coverings to a building, being laminate flooring in some rooms and carpets in others, all of this is within CIS even though carpet fitting on its own is specifically excluded.

To get around this, some subcontractors have issued separate invoices for the different operations. HMRC are aware of this and have said that such invoice splitting should be disregarded when the subcontractor is undertaking both activities under the same contract. This would come to light with a physical inspection of records – if the subcontractor issued two invoices at the same time, specifying the same site on each, then the contractor would be liable for not operating CIS correctly.

This may be argued away under the reg. 9 provisions. What it does do, though, is alert HMRC to collusion by the contractor in practices of which they do not approve and is likely to result in a more detailed inspection.

Law: SI 2005/2045, reg. 9

3.4   Professional activities

It is not intended that CIS applies to professionals, because they never fail to declare their income. Almost never. Architects, surveyors and planning consultants are allowed to be paid gross, do not need to register for CIS and therefore need not feature on the monthly return. This category is extended to include actual operations on the land such as soil and environmental testing and pipeline inspection. This also includes payments to subcontractors for digging.

If the professional's operations also include becoming a developer or involved with hands-on project management or supervision, the exemption is lost.

Planning work undertaken or technical advice provided by a construction manager does not convey any exemption as this would be a normal part of their work.

Guidance: CISR 14270

3.5   End client

Some businesses involved in construction operations have not registered for CIS, either as a subcontractor or contractor, because they believe that as the end client and/or the end beneficiary is not involved in construction, then CIS does not apply. For example, a business making repairs to domestic houses on behalf of an insurance company.

This is incorrect. Irrespective of who pays, the business is involved in construction operations and must register for CIS. It must also register as a CIS contractor if other self-employed workers are engaged.

3.6   Artistic works

These are excluded from CIS, but HMRC are very prescriptive as to what may be regarded as artistic. The example is given of wrought iron gates, which are principally gates and therefore part of a structure, however much their design may be artistic. Ornamental fountains are within CIS in that they are a structure that requires plumbing and a water supply.

Unless commissioned from a separate subcontractor, work such as decorative masonry is likely to be covered by the inclusion clause.

Further details of the definition of artistic works and exclusions can be found at CISR 14080.

Guidance: CIS 14080

3.7   Installation and systems

The principle of a functioning building can be applied to understand which systems and their installation come within CIS. Heating, lighting, ventilation, air conditioning, power supply, drainage, sanitation and water supply are all included.

Other systems without which the building could function, such as security and public address systems, would not be within CIS, though it can depend on the purpose of the building. For a theatre or concert venue, an integrated sound system would be included in CIS.

Lifts and escalators are included, being part of the building's access. Chair lifts are included for similar reasons – not least nowadays that they are designed into the building – but stair lifts, with removable rails that operate in existing stairways, are excluded.

This only applies to the construction of the building. All subsequent repair or maintenance of those systems would be excluded from CIS, even if the replacement item or system represented an improvement in the service provided. An extension of electrical wiring for additional sockets in itself would be excluded, but included if part of more extensive works.

The installation of machinery for use in the building can cause some confusion. If the machinery can be removed, then it is not part of the building and its supply is not within CIS. As for its installation, anything that incorporates the machinery into the building such as bracing structures, or if it is part of a production line, is likely to be within CIS. Anything done to the building by those involved in its construction that enables machinery to be installed, separate to its installation, would be within CIS.

3.8   Cleaning

Until the building is handed over, or once construction operations have been completed, all internal cleaning comes within CIS. Routine cleaning of empty buildings, including those yet to be occupied, is excluded.

Perhaps surprisingly, external cleaning such as shot-blasting is excluded. However, if the same contractor – or work within the same contract – is undertaken to repair the building as a result of the cleaning, then it becomes a mixed contract and is included.

3.9   Miscellaneous operations

The following is a list of operations to clarify those areas that may be contentious or unclear.

Included in CIS:

- fencing (unless an isolated operation and a "light duty structure");
- installation of furniture, including kitchens, bathrooms, bedrooms, cupboards, shelving, shopfitting and racking;

- installation of fire alarm and protection systems;
- floor coverings when part of a construction project, including outdoor surfaces;
- industrial plant built onto the land and not located in a building;
- painting, gilding, varnishing, polishing and ceiling masonry;
- security fencing, gates, bollards and CCTV for traffic management; and
- provision of temporary structures to construction sites, e.g. portable offices.

Excluded from CIS:

- murals;
- temporary structures – film sets, marquees, exhibition stands;
- computer and telephone networks (unless involved with other construction operations);
- fixed seating;
- carpet fitting and floor coverings if not part of a construction project;
- golf courses (if separate from construction of buildings);
- locking systems;
- blinds, curtains and shutters; and
- CCTV for security purposes.

3.10   Overseas territories

Operations taking place partly outside UK territorial waters – such as the construction of a pipeline from an offshore rig to an onshore terminal – would be within CIS.

Section 74(1)(b) states that operations not carried out in the United Kingdom or its territorial sea are not within CIS. However, a subcontractor based overseas but conducting construction operations in the UK for a contractor would be subject to CIS and would therefore need to register accordingly.

That overseas subcontractor would also have to operate CIS for any UK-based subcontractors that it might itself engage.

Any operations conducted by UK businesses overseas, whether for a UK or overseas contractor, would be outside of CIS.

Law: FA 2004, s. 74

3.11   Test case

HMRC's CIS Manual makes a specific reference to the Channel Islands and the Isle of Man as being outside the UK in the context of the scheme. An attempt was made to exploit this as set out in the *Island Contract* case.

Payments to UK workers for work in the UK were routed through an Isle of Man company. The FTT held that the payments to the IoM company should have been made net of CIS tax and upheld the assessments for that tax from the UK company. Two years later, the Upper Tribunal upheld this decision.

Case: *Island Contract Management (UK) Ltd v HMRC* [2013] UKFTT 207 (TC); [2015] UKUT 472 (TCC)

3.12   Reverse premiums

This has been a source of confusion, and will remain so until HMRC issue a definitive statement.

Landlords may make payments to tenants, as an inducement to entering into a lease. That is outside the scope of CIS. There are other circumstances in which landlords may make payments to tenants, and that is where the confusion lies.

Such payments may be as a contribution to basic tenants' works, or for the tenant to undertake works for the landlord. The exemption applies to the former, but the definition of "basic" is unclear.

Some landlords have made CIS deductions from payments to tenants, possibly unnecessarily; others that have not, are concerned that they may be deemed contractors.

The CIOT have suggested in a submission to HMRC that all payments by landlords to tenants should be outside the scope of CIS, extending the pragmatic stance taken for buy-to-let landlords. HMRC have yet to reply.

Law: SI 2005/2045, reg. 20

4. Contractors and subcontractors

4.1 Definitions

A contractor is a business entity that engages another business entity to undertake paid work. That other business entity is a subcontractor.

These are the definitions for CIS. In some industries, a freelancer may term himself a contractor – that is to distinguish him from being an employee. CIS does not concern itself with employees, so the definition above will be used.

Some business entities can be both contractor and subcontractor at the same time. There are often different tiers of engagement in a construction project.

4.2 Mainstream contractor

4.2.1 General principles

These are the businesses that are principally intended to operate CIS. These include businesses that undertake construction work and those that supply labour for construction work.

Within the definition of mainstream contractors are construction businesses, including foreign companies operating in the UK, as well as property developers undertaking work on buildings with a view to profit. However, they are distinct from property investors, unless their undertakings are such that they qualify as deemed contractors.

As well as work on buildings, mainstream contractors include those businesses involved in work on utilities, telecommunications and transport networks and infrastructure.

Gang leaders or gangmasters should also be regarded as mainstream contractors, for those workers that are being supplied who are genuinely self-employed. The same applies to labour agencies supplying workers if the contract for provision of labour to the contractor is with that agency.

The business status of the entity – sole trader or limited company – makes no difference to the definition of contractor and subcontractor. A sole trader may engage a limited company, in which case the company is still the subcontractor to the sole trader contractor.

4.2.2 Example

The end client engages a construction company, A plc to build its new warehouse. That need not make the end client a contractor for CIS – that will be covered later in the chapter.

A plc may engage several other businesses; they may choose to outsource the landscaping, installation of drains or any part of the envelope of the building itself. Let us say that the steel structure of the warehouse is put out to tender and won by B Ltd.

B Ltd becomes a subcontractor to A plc, the contractor. This is the first time that B Ltd has worked for A plc, so A plc has to verify B Ltd for payments under CIS. B Ltd is found to have gross payment status.

B Ltd receives the plans and purchases the steel necessary from Z Ltd. Z Ltd is not a subcontractor of B Ltd, because it is only a supplier of materials.

B Ltd looks at where its activities fit in the proposed time plan for the project. It owns the flatbed lorry to transport the fabricated parts of the steel structure to the site, but not the crane for its installation. B Ltd contacts X plc, a large plant hire company, to arrange for a crane to be on site for the days needed.

At this point, B Ltd may be a contractor. According to the CIS rules, if only the crane is supplied, then X plc is just that – a supplier. If X plc provides a crane operator, then X plc becomes a subcontractor to B Ltd. There is a labour element and therefore this should be shown separately on the invoice from X to B and reported as such on B's monthly CIS return. B has to verify X. B is then both subcontractor (to A plc) and contractor (of X plc).

There are two other scenarios here; if B Ltd's own employees are qualified to operate the crane, then X plc remains only a supplier and not a subcontractor. If B engages a crane operator separately, the crane operator is a subcontractor to B and must be verified. X plc is still only a supplier.

Due to the location and time constraints of the project, B Ltd decides to use two gangs of steel erectors. One will be made up of its own employees. The other will be sourced from a local provider, C, that B Ltd has used before. C is a subcontractor to B Ltd, B Ltd is the contractor of C. B Ltd has paid C within the last two years, so there is no need for verification, but the record shows that C does not hold gross payment status.

C engages all his workers on a self-employed basis. Two of them, D and E, have worked only for C for several years. Alongside these two, C engages F and G to provide a gang of four workers. D, E, F and G are all subcontractors to C. All four have been verified recently by C and are paid net.

To be clear on this, C is not a subcontractor to A plc. His business relationship is with B Ltd. Similarly, D (and E, F and G) are not subcontractors to A plc or B Ltd. Their business relationships are only with C.

The end client makes the first stage payment to A plc. If the end client is not a deemed contractor (covered later in the chapter), then there is no return to be made under CIS.

B Ltd makes its first application for payment to A plc. The quantity surveyor at A plc only approves part of the sum applied for and after making a further deduction for retention, authorises this for payment. That lower sum which is actually paid is entered (net of VAT) on A's monthly CIS return without deduction of tax as a payment to a subcontractor.

B Ltd receives an invoice for the first month from C. All is in order and being labour-only, there are no deductions for materials. Payment is made net of 20% tax to C and a deduction statement is issued. The payment and tax deducted are entered in B's monthly CIS return.

C pays D, E, F and G, having worked out what they are owed, deducts tax and makes the appropriate entries in his monthly CIS return. C might receive invoices from his subcontractors but usually not. C only tends to issue deduction statements when the subbies have their tax returns prepared.

4.2.3   Variations

Example

This example sets out the usual chain of operation. There is no jumping of links unless there is a change and direct link between business entities. If, for example, B Ltd engages the steel erector G directly as a temporary replacement for an ill employee, then G leaves C and is then subcontracting to B Ltd. If in doubt – it is down to who pays whom.

If, after the project is completed, C is investigated by HMRC and is found at a Tax Tribunal to have employed D and E, that makes no difference to the relationship between B Ltd and C. B Ltd engaged C to provide site labour – if those workers are employees or self-employed subcontractors, it does not matter.

D and E, and for that matter HMRC, have no redress against B Ltd. Unless, that is, D and E can prove that C was entirely absent and they were under the supervision, direction and control of B Ltd's staff – and even then, they would only be given employment status, not subcontractor status.

The contractors A plc, B Ltd and C are involved in construction operations as defined by CIS. They are what is known as mainstream contractors.

4.3   Deemed contractors

4.3.1   Definition

What about those not in construction, but who incur costs on operations covered by CIS? The term 'deemed contractors' is used to denote any person carrying on a business, or certain bodies, whose expenditure on construction operations exceeds specified limits.

4.3.2   Private individuals

A homeowner who engages a worker, or a larger business, to undertake work on his house is not a CIS contractor. As in the example above, he is the end client. Domestic work such as this does not fall within CIS.

33

However, there are a few variations of this scenario that are worth considering. The example of the engaged worker asking the homeowner to purchase the materials for the job is often cited – this avoids the worker having to register for VAT. If more than one worker is involved, the principal contact may also ask the homeowner to pay the other worker separately.

In these cases, the homeowner is not a CIS contractor. Even if the homeowner decides to undertake his own project management for an extension or renovation of the property or perhaps a brand new home, engaging a series of workers – that does not bring that work within CIS.

The homeowner is not in the construction business and the work is being undertaken on his own home. These are both specific exemptions from CIS.

Extending that a little, what about buy-to-let landlords, owning a property in which they live, but another which is rented out for gain?

In that circumstance, HMRC have said consistently that buy-to-let landlords are *not* caught by CIS. Even if the property requires a lot of work to make it habitable and legal to let, that does not oblige the property owner to register as a CIS contractor.

However, the HMRC statement was made with the idea of modest property speculation, typically with only one other property owned for rent. What about people who have invested in several properties?

4.3.3   Property investors

The principle is the same. Such individuals are not engaged in construction activities; the properties are essentially investments. That does assume that the multiple landlord has other earnings. If such a person has no other significant income and can be seen to be living off that rental income, then it is possible for HMRC to regard that person as a contractor.

It is not possible to be definitive, as this has yet to be tested in the courts. Nor have HMRC made any statement one way or the other. But given that someone being cared for in his or her own home has to set up a PAYE scheme to pay the careworkers, then the rent-dependent landlord may choose to register and administer his own CIS scheme to be on the safe side.

What if an individual decides to purchase a property with a view to renovating it and selling it for a profit? This is a question that accountants are asked regularly by clients. However tempted by the various reliefs available for capital gains tax, the individual is in that circumstance a property developer – straightaway, first property, no question. And in that circumstance, the person should register for a UTR and then as a CIS contractor, because that is a business venture. There are CGT reliefs available for property transactions, but those do not apply to this situation.

This answer normally leads to some further "what-ifs". Such as, what if I plan to live in it but then change my mind? Or am building it for my eldest child who then decides to live elsewhere? Or for my ageing parent, who later decides they cannot cope?

In those circumstances, the individual would probably have the surplus proceeds on sale classed as a capital gain rather than a trading profit and would also exempt himself from CIS. Unless the individual had erected a for-sale board before work on the property had started.

For larger property investment businesses, the same principle applies until the £1 million threshold is breached. HMRC recognise that such investors will need to spend money on their properties to maintain their value. Anything more substantial than repair or refurbishment, such as the conversion of a large commercial building into flats, would be regarded as the activity of a mainstream contractor.

The issue of whether a property was acquired as part of a trade or as an investment is discussed at length in the case of *Terrace Hill*. There are some useful markers in the transcript, in respect of property trading and finance.

Law: SI 2005/2045, reg. 22
Case: *Terrace Hill (Berkeley) Ltd v HMRC* [2015] UKFTT 75 (TC)
Guidance: CISR 15140

4.3.4   *Businesses*

The guidance can be less than clear, so it is worth beginning with the fact that businesses that are not involved in construction activities are not CIS contractors.

Some businesses commission construction firms to undertake work for them, but the important exemption to note here is that if the work is for the business's own premises, used for the purposes of that business, then the business is not obliged to register or act as a CIS contractor. This exemption applies even if the expenditure is more than £1 million per year.

The exemption covers other companies within the same group, should that situation exist, and any companies under the control of that business. Schools under local authority control also benefit from this exemption.

This covers businesses which own their own properties and also those that rent them under tenant-repairing leases, perhaps undertaking landlord-approved leasehold improvements.

That narrows the field down yet further. So, which non-construction businesses do need to register for CIS?

If a business owns or leases property that is let or sublet to a third party for commercial purposes, or owns property that is for sale or as an investment, then that business must register as a CIS contractor and apply the scheme for any payments for construction work undertaken on those properties.

That applies only to those properties though, not on those used for the purpose of the business – this being covered by the aforementioned exemption.

Regarding the £1 million threshold, HMRC officers are advised in their guidance not to apply CIS to those businesses where construction expenditure fluctuates above and below that level.

There are some other exceptions and inclusions, which require HMRC authorisation:

- deemed contractors need not apply the scheme to payments excluding materials of less than £1,000;

- mainstream contractors need not apply the scheme to payments excluding materials of less than £1,000 on the subcontractor's own premises, or for work on agricultural property of which the subcontractor is a tenant.

That said, it is probably quicker to process the payment net than obtain authorisation from HMRC.

Law: SI 2005/2045, reg. 18, 19

4.3.5 Other entities

Charities need not apply CIS to construction operations, unless the expenditure is incurred by a trading subsidiary of that charity.

In the early days of the current scheme, inspectors in one particular HMRC tax district decided to interpret the definition of deemed contractors, such that if the property was integral to the operation of the business, then that business should register as a CIS contractor. They attempted to levy penalties for a couple of businesses that they considered to be non-compliant.

This was not thought to be a sensible approach. This would have brought tens of thousands of businesses within CIS. This was not adopted by HMRC.

Local authorities, NHS trusts and public offices are included as deemed contractors should their construction expenditure exceed the £1m threshold. Public – i.e. private – schools would also be included under the same criteria, unless they have charitable status.

Law: SI 2005/2045, reg. 21-24

4.3.6 Groups of companies

Within such groups, it is only companies that undertake construction operations that become CIS contractors. This can be the case if work is being undertaken on behalf of other group companies, to avoid duplication of registration.

4.3.7 Occasional subcontractors

Sat between the trades that are definitely within the scope of CIS and others that are definitely outside, are those businesses which will occasionally need to be paid within CIS.

Therefore it makes sense to read through the section of CIS340 that refers to the scope of construction operations included in the scheme. Even then, it is not always crystal clear.

Take the section that refers to the installation of systems. Specifically mentioned is heating and lighting, and most people would think that such a facility was a prerequisite for a functional building. This also includes telephone and internet cabling installation.

Therefore a business that supplies and installs telephone systems to offices for many different trades will have no contact with CIS – unless it is making such an installation in a building for a property developer, in which case it needs to be registered for CIS. Its gross payment status will depend on its size and compliance record, any deduction being recoverable from SA or PAYE accordingly.

The definition has evolved with time, but the best way to understand it is to think of what a building needs for its workers or inhabitants; the core shell of the building, windows, heat, light and communications.

Amongst the exclusions are artistic works, signs, security systems, fixed seating and window blinds. They may be desirable but are not regarded (for CIS) as necessary. Also excluded are carpets; some floor covering is necessary, but carpets are not. Unless their fitting is part of a mixed contract, in which case it is all included.

5. Verification

5.1 Introduction

CIS can only work as intended if the workers or businesses that are being paid, are correctly identified.

5.2 Earlier methods

The original 1972 scheme did not achieve that, so in 1975 the system of 714 cards and SC60 deductions was introduced. This did work largely as intended until in the late 1990s it was felt that there was too easy a trade in 714s and that gross payment status was being too readily granted.

The revisions to the scheme in 1999 brought about the CIS4, 5 and 6 cards.

The CIS4 card still meant deduction of tax, but did verify the worker and provide his UTR. The greater problem arose with the CIS6 cards.

If the business had GPS but was not large enough to warrant CIS5 status, then one of the representatives of the business – a CIS6 cardholder – had to present that card to the administrative office of the contractor, not to the site foreman.

In many cases, this meant a round trip of several hundred miles merely to present a card, the act of a few seconds. Sometimes the contractor would be open to receiving a copy of the card by post or fax, but such was the fear of non-compliance, that "by the book" was considered rather safer.

Regrettably, the people who drew up the book did not think this through or did not care about the waste of time. This was one of the reasons that the proposals for what is now the current scheme began to be drafted relatively soon – in 2002 – after the revisions introduced in August 1999.

This gave us what we have now, which is the requirement to engage HMRC in the verification of subcontractors and by the production of the V-number to prove that correct procedure has been followed.

Subbies with CIS4 cards were told to destroy them, which was something of a regressive step as they were a useful way for the worker to provide his UTR. This was probably a bureaucratic way of moving everyone involved onto the new scheme, but also an attempt to shift the mindset of the industry away from the idea of "I have a card therefore I must be self-employed". Possession of a UTR was thought to be less tangible than a card, which conveyed similar status to a CSCS card.

5.3   Current system

5.3.1   *Before verification*

The HMRC guidance states that before making a first payment, the contractor should be satisfied that the engagement is one of self-employment. Suggestions are made of contacting HMRC or using the Employment Status Indicator (ESI). This is guidance and not law, and of course there are other sources of advice. Nothing is stipulated as to how this satisfaction should be documented.

5.3.2   *Making a verification*

HMRC's system is set up so this should be made online. This can be by use of its own software or that of a commercial provider. See notes below about telephone verification.

The current system of verification demands that when a contractor engages a subcontractor for the first time, the name and UTR need to be obtained, together with the NI number for sole traders, or the company registration number for companies. The verification can still be made if the NI number has not yet been issued.

Contact must then be made with HMRC. The rate of deduction applicable will be advised – 0%, 20% or 30% – and a verification number will be provided. This will be in the form of a reference V plus ten digits.

There are no restrictions as to who may make the verification. As long as the person contacting HMRC has the contractor name and a tax reference – which can be the PAYE reference or a UTR, just so long as the contractor is still active – then the verification can be made. That person will be asked to identify himself, in the capacity in which the verification is being made. The question will be asked for each subcontractor, whether a tender has been made, a contract signed or a work order generated.

The HMRC guidance for verifying partnerships is a little peculiar. A partnership is likely to have a business bank account in its name, to receive online payments and into which cheques (in the partnership name) and cash may be paid in. However the guidance refers to persons being paid on behalf of the partnership; if all partners can receive such payments, each of the partners' UTRs will be requested in addition to that of the partnership.

For subcontractors paid gross or at 20%, there is no need to enter the verification reference on the monthly return – only if the higher rate is applicable. It is recommended that a record is kept of the references.

The verification holds good for a minimum of two years. If a subcontractor was paid in the month to 5 May 2016, that counts as a payment in 2016-17. If the next payment to that subcontractor is not until 5 April 2019 (i.e. 2018-19), there would be no need to re-verify as the original verification was within the last two years.

However if a subbie was paid in the month ended 5 April 2016 (in 2015-16) and not again until the month ended 5 May 2018 (2018-19), then re-verification would be necessary.

So in some circumstances, it is not necessary to re-verify for 35 months, but absolutely vital to re-verify after 25 months. Clear? It had better be, as this could be a non-compliance reason for GPS revocation.

For groups of companies, if a subcontractor has been verified by one of those companies within the qualifying time period, it is not necessary for any of the other group companies to do so if paying that same subcontractor.

5.3.3   Higher rate of deduction

The reference will be amended with a suffix where the deduction needs to be made at the higher rate, so it becomes something like V1122334455/A. This has to be shown on the deduction statement given to the subcontractor only when the higher rate is applied. It also needs to be entered on the CIS monthly return.

The higher rate applies where HMRC are unable to verify the subcontractor. This may be because the subcontractor is not registered with HMRC – in which case 30% is thought to be a safe amount to recoup as tax, should that subbie decide never to register.

The reason for the higher rate being specified may also be that incorrect details have been given – the UTR, NI or company number, but also the exact spelling of the name of the subcontractor. This latter incidence has increased with the influx of workers from other countries.

In practice, the application of the higher rate of deduction has been fairly low – between 1 and 2 percent of all verifications. This would have been higher had it not been for the provision of the telephone service for verification.

If the name of the subcontractor does not match exactly with the HMRC registration details, then the answer is "unmatched – 30%". What normally then happened is that the person at the contractor's office telephoned HMRC and common sense applied, if the number references matched but that there was a small discrepancy in the spelling of the name. The expected answer would then be given – 0 or 20% deduction – and a new verification reference provided, with the previous reference ignored.

The telephone service had been widely used, forming nearly half of all verifications, whether for the reason given above, or because some contractors' staff prefer to talk to a human being, or because the internet connection is slow or unavailable.

Which makes it all the more surprising that HMRC chose to do away with it.

5.3.4   *Changes in the provision of service*

In the 2014 consultation, the question was asked regarding the impact of removing this option and how any difficulties could be overcome. The reported answers included the need for the current online system to be improved in respect of providing a reason for an unmatched verification and to allow for minor misspellings – described as "fuzzy name matching". The consensus was that there should be no change in the current service until those improvements had been made and proven to work.

The official response was that the withdrawal of the telephone service would be delayed until 2017. This would allow time for the IT technicians to amend the current system. However, a reduced service would be retained for "non-routine" cases and for contractors unable to access online services. In other words, another part of the HMRC system where you sit on the phone for half an hour.

It is difficult to see how the removal of a service helps towards the reduction of administrative burdens, to which apparently HM Government is committed. It also makes you wonder how HMRC defines service.

5.3.5 Current service provisions

The online verification system is now fully operational. This is HMRC's preferred method for contractors. There is a telephone service available, but this is intended for unusual circumstances. It is unclear how well resourced this back-up system will be, but it has been stated by HMRC that there should be no outright refusal to verify a subcontractor by telephone. It may require some insistence as to why a telephone verification is necessary, but it will be achieved in the end.

Law: SI 2005/2045, reg. 6

5.4 Changes in concern

If a subcontractor has a change in business concern, such as a sole trader becoming a partnership or incorporating, then each contractor with whom the subbie deals should be advised, with the new references as applicable. This could otherwise cause problems for contractors, especially if GPS is involved.

It is sensible for the contractor to ask the question regarding any change in trading status, should a subcontractor provide different bank details.

As part of an initiative to reduce fraud in construction, it has been proposed that contractors should regularly check the ownership of subcontractor trading entities. This has yet to be made mandatory, or indeed detailed as to the required actions.

If a contractor changes business concern, a new scheme will need to be established and all subcontractors paid from that point will need to be re-verified. However this would not be necessary for the takeover of an existing business such that the established scheme is maintained.

In the event of a sole-trader subcontractor dying, but with the intention for the business to continue, the new owners will need to re-register. The existing scheme may continue in the interim but the executors should advise HMRC.

5.5   Subcontractors based overseas

If a contractor engages a subcontractor that has no base in the UK, then CIS must apply. The rate of deduction will be 30%, as there will be no UTR to check. It is important that contractors are aware of this, as failure to process payments to such subcontractors through CIS could open them up to assessment of tax not deducted, as well as penalties for not applying the scheme.

Case: *Schotten and Hansen (UK) Ltd v HMRC* [2017] UKFTT 191 (TC)

6. Agents and CIS

6.1 Introduction

For many years, it has been a source of frustration for those in HMRC administering CIS, that there has been a steadfast refusal by their colleagues to allow form 64-8 to have a specific CIS section for authorising agents to act on behalf of their contractor clients.

For agents managing CIS affairs, this has meant that relationships with HMRC are less clear, and there have been many instances of refusals by HMRC to deal with agents for lack of authorisation. There is no automatic cross-over for CIS, for agents already authorised to deal with other taxes for their clients. This is despite the guidance for HMRC officers in CISR90060 that says there is.

6.2 Correct procedure

On the paper version of form 64-8, the authorisation section for PAYE asks for the employer and accounts office references, and for SA or CT references. For those using that paper form, the HMRC guidance says that for CIS authorisation, the authorising party should make a clear note on the form or attach a separate letter.

For agents that will be making submissions on behalf of contractors online, which soon will be all of them, form FBI2 is more specific and has the provision to authorise an agent for PAYE, or CIS, or both.

HMRC distinguish these two instances as Customer Level Agents (CLA – who will also deal with the SA or CT affairs of the contractor) and Scheme Specific Agents (SSA). A contractor may have a different agent to deal solely with CIS. Both cannot be authorised for CIS at the same time.

Notification of authorised agents can also be made on forms CIS301, 302, 304 and 305 as mentioned at **2.1.2** above.

6.3 Representation

An authorised agent can represent the contractor when providing information to HMRC, or raising queries on their client's behalf. If the agent is to receive paper monthly returns, a specific written request or call to the CIS helpline needs to be made.

It is best that the agent is registered with HMRC as a PAYE/CIS agent, with the appropriate reference. An unregistered agent can submit a CIS return on behalf of a contractor, but cannot then correct any errors or make subcontractor verifications, or use the HMRC software. If the agent is an already-registered CLA, an additional authorisation for CIS will need to be submitted.

If the agent uses the online authorisation system, having entered the contractor's PAYE and accounts office references, HMRC will issue an authorisation code to the contractor, marked CS for CIS submissions. The agent will need this to be fully authorised for CIS for that contractor. This code can take some days to arrive, which is something worth noting if the restriction of filing-only is to be avoided.

7. Gross payment status

7.1 Introduction

For most businesses, being paid all that is invoiced is normal. For businesses in the construction industry, it is a privilege – according to Dawn Primarolo MP, who approved the beginnings of what is the current scheme.

Without becoming involved in discussions over retentions and sums applied for but not authorised, it is possible for construction businesses to receive all that is invoiced or applied for. But, in the eyes of HMRC, this is not the normal state of affairs – as stated in CIS340, subcontractors can apply to be paid gross, the assumption being that they should be paid net of tax.

Those businesses just have to be big enough and sufficiently compliant.

7.2 How to qualify for GPS

7.2.1 Business test

It is necessary for the business to be registered with HMRC, and also registered for CIS. There needs to be a business bank account in place and a business address. Construction operations, or supplying labour for such operations, need to have been conducted in the UK.

HMRC are able to check that bank account details are correct, with the use of a "Bank Wizard". This can be an account that is used for private and business banking, so long as it is a current account.

In the case of a business that has been run from home, it may be a good idea to submit with the application, additional information to substantiate the existence of a *bona fide* business, such as copies of invoices and receipts for materials or plant hire. HMRC have to be sure that a business is in existence.

Law: SI 2005/2045, reg. 27

7.2.2   *Turnover test*

It used to be the case that any subcontractor could receive a 714 and be paid gross, irrespective of the level of turnover. That changed when the scheme was revised in 1999. A minimum turnover level was introduced of £30,000 per sole trader, per partner in the case of partnerships, or per director for limited companies. This sum represents labour billed, therefore excluding materials, and net of VAT.

Also introduced was, for businesses with multiple partners or directors, a minimum threshold of £200,000, which was reduced in April 2016 to £100,000.

This is the case for businesses already in existence and registered for CIS. HMRC will accept copies of accounts – which may need to be re-stated, depending on which expenses have been included in cost of sales. It is necessary to show that £30,000 of labour per principal (let us call them) has been billed and declared, so excluding subcontract labour and any attributed overheads from cost of sales, we are essentially looking at £30,000 of gross profit per principal.

What about new businesses? HMRC will grant GPS straightaway, but it would be necessary to prove that the turnover threshold will be exceeded very quickly, and this is only available to companies and partnerships. Turnover to date of £30,000 and a copy of a signed contract or contracts for no less than £200,000, with the applicant subcontractor named as such, would be accepted. Otherwise, it is a case of doing the work and applying when the business is big enough. No *pro rata* calculation is made for part-time workers.

There are provisions for businesses taking over other construction businesses to qualify for GPS, on the basis of "inherited" or "transferred" receipts. The same limits apply but the aggregate turnover may allow for an application. However, the compliance test rules will be applied to the previous business owner, to prevent incorporation creating a clean slate.

What sort of work qualifies? Could a business put up three or four conservatories in the unregulated domestic market and then apply for GPS? Yes – such qualifying operations for private householders may be included in the turnover stated. Could two businesses simply charge each other £31,000? No, as this would fail in the event of the information being checked and could bring about a penalty charge. As part of their procedures, HMRC will check their existing information from SA and CT returns for turnover and materials declared previously.

That said, the application form needs to be completed and posted, so it is recommended that accounts are sent with it as a backup and also to indicate which annual period constitutes the attainment of the threshold. The application rules are that the twelve month period should be up to the date of application, so some management accounts may be needed to supplement earlier annual accounts.

Referring back to turnover within the construction industry, this includes any business that has been paid net. Therefore an agency providing labour to a contractor is specifically included, even though its owners could run the business from a spare bedroom and never see a construction site. Granting such operations GPS has proved costly to HMRC in the past.

Businesses that trade mostly outside, but occasionally within, the scope of construction operations, may apply for GPS if their main turnover exceeds the limits and if future construction receipts are incidental to the main business.

Law: SI 2005/2045, reg. 28-31

7.2.3   Compliance tests

Your business is established, it has made the appropriate registrations and has achieved the required level of turnover. Does that entitle the business to receive all its earnings without deduction of tax? Not automatically, no.

Because you are in construction, HMRC do not trust you. The misdeeds of more than 40 years ago continue to tarnish the industry. In all other trades, you can be as non-compliant as you like and suffer as many penalties as you can bear, and that will not affect your cash flow. Construction is different.

To be granted the privilege of gross payment status, your business has to demonstrate that your record of tax compliance is good. And for good, read nigh on perfect.

In the twelve months to the date of the application, your business must have made all tax submissions and payments within the required deadlines.

For PAYE & NI submissions, however they necessarily occur, these are taken care of by the RTI system. Therefore a contractor business that employs all its labour will have no CIS returns to make or by which to be judged.

Following the 2014 CIS consultation, from April 2016 directors' filing records will not be taken into account, nor will payment of P11d tax, SA or CT liabilities.

The business also needs to have made its tax payments on time. Principally, PAYE & NI, but also the P11d liability, CT and/or SA tax. In the past, GPS applications had been denied (initially) for a director reducing SA payments on account, and needing to make a balancing payment.

Significantly excluded, though, is VAT. CIS does not recognise this in its review of compliance. This is probably a throwback to the days before the merger of the Inland Revenue and Customs & Excise, in that the Revenue still regard the VAT lot as the poor relation. The official explanation is likely to refer to access to computer systems, despite the fact that PAYE and VAT inspectors regularly accompany each other on taxpayer inspections.

Is there any leeway in the compliance tests? Yes. When the application for GPS for the business is made, the HMRC systems will review its records of submission and payment. These are called Tax Treatment Qualifying Tests, or TTQT. Silence implies satisfaction, so if any defalcation falls within the parameters set within the TTQT system, nothing will be reported.

These are the levels of tolerance.

PAYE & NI, and CIS

Payments

- Three late payments of more than £100 up to 14 days late are permitted. Four such payments – FAILURE.

- Any payment of more than £100 more than 14 days after the due date – FAILURE.
- Any payment of more than £100 still unpaid at the date of application – FAILURE.

Submissions

- Three late submissions of the CIS monthly return up to 28 days late are permitted. Four such late submissions – FAILURE.
- Any submission of the monthly return more than 28 days late – FAILURE.
- Any submission of the monthly return still outstanding at the date of application – FAILURE.

Class 1A NIC

Payments

- A late payment of £100 within 14 days of the due date of 19 July is permitted. Any such payment later than that – FAILURE.

Self assessment

Payments

- Any payment of less than £100 is disregarded. One late payment of more than £100 is permitted. Two such late payments – FAILURE.
- Any penalty levied on the late submission of an SA return is not a problem, but payment of that penalty after the due date – FAILURE.
- Any SA liability of more than £100 still outstanding at the date of application – FAILURE.

Submissions

- Late submissions of SA returns are no longer taken into account, unless any are outstanding at the date of application, in which case – FAILURE.

Corporation tax

Payments

- Any payment of more than £100 is allowed to be up to 28 days late, even if it accrues interest. Any such payment made more than 28 days late – FAILURE.
- Any payment of more than £100 still outstanding at the date of application – FAILURE.

Submissions

- Late submissions of CT returns are no longer taken into account, unless any are outstanding at the date of application, in which case – FAILURE.

Clearly, it makes a lot of sense to be sure nothing is outstanding when the application is made or during the period taken for its process.

An application can still be made if a Time to Pay arrangement is still in existence. If DMB report that the promised payments have been made on time, this need not affect the GPS application. However, this is likely to be provisional and any subsequent late payment could lead to an immediate GPS withdrawal.

The twelve month qualifying period is intended to involve a review of the applicant's tax history during that time. It is sensible to offer information to fill in any gaps, such as a period spent abroad, unemployed, in hospital or in full-time education.

If your application as an initial GPS registration has failed, that is it. The HMRC review inspectors have no powers of judgment or discretion in this instance. You can reapply in no less than twelve months' time (known as the exclusion period), at the end of which time the same tests will be applied to the most recent period.

Part of the compliance test involves looking for possible shadow directors. For a company with only one director, it may be suspected that others are involved but that declaring just one passes the turnover test – but also that one of those others are known to HMRC and not in a good way. Questions may be asked if suspicions are raised that the company's principal may not be involved in construction, or if an address is shared with a known offender, or if a virtual office address is used.

Law: SI 2005/2045, reg. 32-36

7.2.4   Identification

HMRC may require the GPS applicants to provide details of identity in support of the registration. The application may fail if it is thought that incorrect information has been provided.

Also note that, as set out in **2.1.6**, penalties can be levied against businesses providing false information, either recklessly or knowingly.

Law: SI 2005/2045, reg. 25

7.3   Process of registration

The current HMRC procedure is to make registration by telephone by an authorised officer of the business, or by completing the online form and sending it in (with appropriate enclosures) to HMRC, currently to the Swansea office.

After granting GPS, HMRC randomly select a number of businesses that will be asked to substantiate the information provided in the application. Therefore it is sensible to retain any workings used to calculate the turnover net of materials figure provided. Evidence required will include deduction statements, bank statements and copies of invoices issued to non-CIS clients.

The cover-all penalty provision of up to £3,000 applies to applications where the figures have been deliberately misrepresented.

7.4   Retention of gross payment status

7.4.1   Coverage

There are about 100,000 construction businesses with GPS. From the statistics around the time of the launch of the current scheme in 2007, the failure rate was 30%. That was not always enforced and though HMRC resources no longer allow detailed record-keeping, the loss after appeals is now reckoned – by HMRC – to be around 5%.

7.4.2   Annual reviews

HMRC aim to review all businesses with GPS annually. The review date is not linked to the tax year or the accounting year end, but the list of businesses is spread by HMRC. The intention is that a scheduled review takes place at least once each year, so the date of a review may move forward each year.

A review can be requested manually at any time by an authorised HMRC officer. The system will also self-generate a review in the event of several compliance failures, before the scheduled date. This is to inform HMRC that failures of sufficient severity may warrant an immediate withdrawal of GPS – subject to reasonable excuse and appeal.

If your business passes the TTQTs, there will be no communication from HMRC; the only way that you will know that a review has taken place is if a failure is recorded.

7.4.3   Sound procedures

To retain GPS, a business has to make sure that all of the submissions and payments included in the tests listed above are made by the due dates.

Late payment may be allowed if a Time to Pay arrangement has been agreed with HMRC. Make sure that such an arrangement is confirmed in writing and that any communication or call reference from HMRC is kept somewhere safe.

You do need to think ahead about this. If you are relying on a client's payment being made by a promised date, to be able to make a tax payment, remember that the HMRC inspectors are directed to view shortage of funds as NOT a reasonable excuse for late payment. Give yourself a cut-off date, and if the money has not arrived by then, contact HMRC ahead of the date and ask for a Time to Pay arrangement. Have an offer date in mind before you make the call.

If you are still writing cheques for tax payments and insist on doing so, then obtaining proof of delivery is a good idea. As this means traipsing to a post office and waiting in a queue, you might want to reconsider this.

Postal delays can be accepted as a reasonable excuse – once. Sad to say, the post office is less reliable than it was, so it is best to avoid the problem occurring.

7.4.4   Extent of the review

There will be no turnover test included in the review. This is because of the rules regarding the scope of CIS. Some businesses may only occasionally work in areas covered by the definition of construction – for example, a company selling and installing telecommunication systems. Only if that company is involved in the cabling of a new building will they be treated as a CIS subcontractor, and may undertake several or no such jobs in a year. That does not prevent them from retaining their GPS.

There is one more test that is now part of the HMRC inspection procedure, though not part of the TTQT review, that – if failed – could lead to loss of GPS, and in some cases has already done so.

A contractor is obliged to provide subcontractors with deduction statements, setting out clearly the sum of tax deducted under CIS. This should be either monthly, or with each payment if less frequently than that. HMRC have been aware that since the revocation of the unsuccessful voucher system in 2007, not all contractors have been fulfilling their obligations in this regard.

This was causing a lot of problems for subcontractors, where it was unclear how much tax had been deducted. This will be addressed in more detail in a later chapter, but for now, it is recommended that full compliance in this area is maintained and can be demonstrated. Round sum payments on account may be convenient, but potentially costly in the long run.

Finally, in the event of a major failure in compliance or payment, HMRC may withdraw GPS at any time. As part of the drive against loss of tax from fraud, this may also occur with the involvement (overt or perceived) in the business of individuals with a poor tax record or convictions.

7.5   Assumed GPS

Where local authorities and other public bodies act as subcontractors, they are not registered for CIS and are therefore assumed to hold GPS, so no deductions should be made from payments made to them. A full list of the public bodies can be found on CISR13040, which is reproduced as **Appendix 4**.

7.6   Change in ownership

Where there is a change in the ownership of a business, the new business must apply to HMRC for GPS in its own right. If a sole trader sells a construction business with GPS, then even if the name of the business is retained, the new owner must make his own application.

The same applies if instead of selling, a sole trader with GPS incorporates his business; an application must be made for the company. The same will apply should a GPS company sell its business to an individual sole trader.

Should two GPS sole traders enter into partnership (rather than a joint venture for a single project), or a GPS sole trader take on a partner, then there is no transfer of status and the partnership must apply to HMRC.

A partnership may retain its GPS if taking on a third partner, though HMRC need to be informed and the turnover of the new business should be reviewed for the current rules and those to come in 2016. Two partnerships with GPS merging into one will similarly have to make a new application and review.

ıll

8.   Potential loss of gross payment status

8.1   Introduction

One day, out of the blue, a letter arrives from the HMRC compliance office in Glasgow, telling you that a review for CIS has been undertaken of your business, and that one or more compliance failures have been registered. Your business is at risk of having its gross payment status revoked by HMRC.

This is the beginning of the first of three 30 day cycles. The letter will tell you that you have 30 days to reply, to provide an explanation for the failure.

Law: SI 2005/2045, reg. 26

8.2   What needs to be done?

After a few deep breaths, reassure yourself that presently, your business still has GPS. The earliest it can be revoked is 90 days after the date of issue of the letter.

The next thing to do is to check through your records of submission and payment. Is the failure listed correct? If you deal with your own monthly CIS returns, then the online records can be checked, though you might have more of a problem if you are still filing paper returns. Check HMRC's recorded date of receipt with your own record of posting.

If there is a failure of submission due to agents that you have engaged, ask for their records of the respective dates. If the failure is down to them, warn them that they may be facing a claim against their professional insurance.

For payments, check the date of despatch with the date recorded of receipt. If payment is by cheque, establish when it was sent. This may not be the date the cheque was written.

Having established the facts, you are now ready for the next stage.

8.3   How to reply

Without delay. Establish the facts and reply; HMRC procedures are that after day 55 of the date of issue of the notification, if no appeal has been received, letters will be produced and sent to all your contractor clients, advising them that from day 90 after the notification, you move from gross status to net. You still have GPS until day 90, and revised letters will be sent by HMRC to your clients in the event of a "late" appeal, but it is best to head off those first letters.

The computer has said no, but your reply to the letter will be read by a person. This will be a trained HMRC inspector who has the power to exercise judgment.

What this inspector has to do is to read your explanation for the failure and assess whether the reasons may be regarded as a reasonable excuse. It may be that the HMRC records are incorrect, or that a payment was made but with an incorrect reference. If this can be proved, then send whatever evidence you can find to prove your case – for example, a bank statement showing the date of presentation of the payment (albeit to a DMB suspense account).

If the failure is one of timing around the 14 or 28 day cut-off deadline, set out clearly the dates of despatch together with whatever proof you can present.

If a late payment is due to a Time to Pay arrangement, this is something that the letter expressly asks for. Send off copies of the evidence for this and point out that there has been no compliance failure.

Let us say that there has been no error in the HMRC review. How do you convince the inspector that you should be let off?

To establish this, we need to study the guidelines on reasonable excuse.

8.4   What is a reasonable excuse?

8.4.1   Guidance

The guidelines for this area for HMRC inspectors to follow are set out in the CIS manual, on pages CISR81030 to 81120. The thing to remember here is that HMRC expect your business to be compliant and to take that obligation seriously.

Sole traders and husband-and-wife businesses are specifically recognised. Sometimes there can be only one person dealing with the tax compliance of a business and that should not deny that business GPS – unless there is a track record of not being able to cope. That, at least, is the official view.

For larger businesses, if there is one member of staff dealing with CIS, then there needs to be a contingency plan in place for his or her holiday, illness or sudden departure. For any business, an existing condition is expected to be managed rather than regularly invoked as an excuse.

The leeway in the TTQT review allows for someone with the sniffles or whether the dog ate your CIS return. Hence, the 14 and 28 day tolerances, which are intended to allow for human error. If any of those are breached, then to pass the reasonable excuse test, something very serious needs to have occurred. This means at least a serious illness, or a chain of illness affecting covering staff where there is more than one administrator in the office. Floods, IT failures and burglaries are also mentioned. However, there is no mention of malicious intent by an unhappy employee. That could easily happen, but is difficult to judge how it may be regarded as an excuse.

Postal delays or indeed disappearance of the item can be accepted – once. HMRC will assume that given the hassle arising from something going missing, the business concerned will find a more reliable method of making submissions.

8.4.2   The inspector's view

The person reading your letter has the task of deciding whether the circumstances set out, that gave rise to the compliance failure, constitute a reasonable excuse. That person is not there to pass judgment on or to be particularly sympathetic to the vagaries of the construction industry and their impact on your business. Is the explanation a reasonable excuse, yes or no?

What you need to do, is to persuade that person on that basis. You will be asked for documentary evidence – so send in copies of doctor's notes, statements from the individual concerned confirming reasons for absence, loss adjuster's reports, photographic evidence – whatever you can to back up your claim and to demonstrate that the circumstances were exceptional.

Let us say that your case is a little on the weak side. It will not hurt to set out what steps have been taken to prevent this happening again – not least actually to prevent it, but also to demonstrate that the matter is being taken seriously in your office.

Clearly, threatening the inspector will not be effective. However, it may not be a bad idea to mention that the potential effect of loss of GPS is so serious that referring the matter to a Tax Tribunal will be inevitable, should the case of the business fail at this stage.

This is not an easy one to judge. The inspector may think, no skin off my nose, and make the decision that there is no reasonable excuse and that GPS should be revoked. In other words, follow procedure, let those higher up deal with it or let the company suffer the consequences.

Alternatively, that person may not wish his decision to be scrutinised at that higher level. Remember, though, that each inspector will have dealt with a lot of cases and will have determined for himself or herself where the boundaries lay. Assume that inspectors are consistent and that they will have received feedback following the outcome of any legal decisions.

If there is nothing else for it than to say, sorry, we forgot – then still reply to the letter. It does you no harm to be seen to be following procedure.

Finally, whatever you do, make sure the letter is sent registered delivery.

8.4.3   The inspector's decision

If the explanation for the compliance failure is considered reasonable, then you will receive a positive reply within thirty days with this decision. Your GPS will not be affected and none of your contractor clients will be any the wiser. HMRC will retain the case on their records, to be taken into account in the event of another failure arising from a future review and to guard against the same marginal excuse being trotted out.

The inspector may not agree with you. Your excuse is not considered to be reasonable and the decision is that GPS should be revoked. Again, HMRC have thirty days to reply. This is the second of the three 30 day cycles.

If you consider that the case is unlikely to be won, then there is no need to reply and, as will be advised, GPS will be revoked at the end of the final 30 day period. All clients with whom your business has worked will be advised that payments should henceforth be made after deduction of tax. Any new clients, when they verify your business as a subcontractor, will be advised that 20% tax should be deducted from the labour content of payments made.

From the date of GPS revocation, an application for re-registration of GPS cannot be made for twelve complete months.

If you want to contest the decision, what do you do?

8.4.4   Internal review

Once the inspector's letter has been received, you have 30 days to reply and to request an internal review. This means that an inspector of the same level as the original assessor – known as the review officer – will review the recorded failure, your explanation as to how it happened and the notes made in respect of the decision to revoke GPS for lack of a reasonable excuse.

If you have additional information to present, or if the wording of your original letter was unclear or presented the facts in a less than constructive way, then say so now. It is unlikely that presented with the same facts, another inspector will arrive at a different conclusion. Again, make sure your letter is sent registered delivery – a lack of response entitles HMRC to assume you accept the decision.

Should you request an internal review, HMRC have 45 days from the date of receipt of your letter to conduct it. Your GPS remains in place while this is done. If the decision is reversed, all well and good; again, no-one knows that any review has taken place and all payments are made gross as before.

If the decision is upheld, you can accept it either in writing or by not replying. The outcome is the same – GPS is lost on receipt of your letter or expiry of the 45 day period, and the twelve month minimum loss period begins.

This is as far as HMRC's internal procedures go. If you wish to contest the decision, the next step is to go to court.

8.5   First-tier Tax Tribunal

If you wish, you can miss out the internal review and advise HMRC that the case is to be taken to a Tax Tribunal. Either way, you need to advise HMRC that you are taking this action, within 30 days of the receipt of the original decision or the outcome of the internal review. Do not change your mind and apply to the Tax Tribunal having asked for an internal review and while it is being conducted.

You will retain your gross payment status throughout this time – in the period while a date for the Tax Tribunal is being organised, and in the period up to the actual date of the Tribunal hearing.

Going to court is a big decision. There will be the costs of whichever agents or legal representation you engage. There will be the time taken in gathering together evidence to fight your case and meeting with your representatives to clarify facts. There will be time taken worrying about the outcome.

Set against this is the alternative, which is the effect on cash flow on being paid net, but more significantly the potential loss of business.

In preparing for your hearing, **Chapter 17** is intended to be of use in analysing past cases concerning loss or denial of GPS and how the findings may apply to your circumstances.

In the event of HMRC's decision being upheld at FTT, an appeal can be made for the case to be heard at the Upper Tribunal. Permission for this has to be sought, but GPS is still retained until it is denied, and retained until the case is re-heard.

9. Penalties

9.1 Introduction

Arguably the most punitive penalty is for HMRC to remove the gross payment status of a business. As this is covered elsewhere, let us consider the quantifiable penalties levied by HMRC for non-compliance with CIS.

This will not cover those penalties levied under RTI, nor the compliance tests that result in loss of GPS.

9.2 History

Up to 1999, there were no penalties levied on businesses specifically for CIS. Between 1999 and 2007, there was a general penalty of up to £3,000 that could be charged for various elements of non-compliance. The old CIS guidance IR14 makes reference to penalty proceedings, without being specific.

From the commencement of the current scheme, a fixed regime of penalties was set out, to take effect from 6 October 2007 – a six month bedding-in period having been granted.

For the late submission of a CIS return – that is, after the 19th of the month – a penalty of £100 was charged. Should that same return not have been submitted by the 19th of the following month, another £100 was charged, and again for all subsequent months.

Therefore, if from commencement (or recognition of the need to register as a contractor) a whole year's returns were not submitted, the business stood to be charged £7,800 (12 x £100 for the first month, 11 x £100 for the second month, and so on).

HMRC seemed quite happy to let their computers churn out these penalty notices. In April 2007, there were about 176,000 active CIS contractors, this being the height of the construction boom.

In the years following, this gave rise to a colossal amount apparently owed to HMRC. Part of the problem was their own database. Concerns had been expressed regarding this in the months preceding April 2007, to be met by reassurance. Notices were being sent out to incorrect addresses. Other notices were accumulating at empty premises, where the database had not been updated for business closures or where the business owners had simply not informed HMRC.

By the middle of 2011, £217 million of unpaid penalty notices had been issued. Against these, HMRC had collected £10 million. They had also written off more than £60 million, raised against defunct businesses or in error. At that time, they were confident of collecting the remainder.

In its 2012-13 Annual Report, HMRC declared the write-off of £220 million of CIS fines.

The accumulation method, where it actually applied, was regarded as excessively punitive. Therefore from October 2011, a revised set of penalties came into force, this time being partially geared to the sum not declared to HMRC.

9.3   Current penalty regime

The CIS monthly return should be submitted such that it is received by HMRC 14 days after the month end. Therefore a return for the month ended 5 January 2018 should be with HMRC no later than 19 January 2018.

The current list of penalties is as follows:

- a return submitted late – £100
- a return submitted two months late – another £200
- a return submitted six months late – another £300 or 5% of the deductions, whichever is greater
- a return submitted twelve months late – another £300 or 5% of the deductions, whichever is greater.

So, a contractor that forgets to file a return for twelve months showing £100 of deductions will be charged £900 in penalties. A contractor in the same position, but showing £10,000 of deductions will be charged £1,300.

A year's worth of £100 returns would come to £5,600, down from £7,800 under the previous method.

If a return is later than twelve months, HMRC have the option to impose an additional penalty of up to £3,000, or 100% of the CIS deductions on the return, whichever is higher.

For contractors that have never filed a CIS return, there are caps that have to be applied to the amounts of £100 and £200 penalties. This amount cannot exceed £3,000, from the date of the first late return to the final late return month. This only applies for the first period of late continuous filing. Capping does not apply to tax-geared penalties. There are some useful examples in the CIS Manual at CISR 65080.

The 5% charge will apply in most cases, when the contractor's behaviour is considered not to be deliberate, but this may increase dependent on the findings of the HMRC officers. If the contractor's behaviour is considered to be deliberate but not concealed, the rate rises to 70%. If considered to be deliberate and concealed, the rate will be 100%. For closer definitions of these terms, which also apply to late returns of other tax schemes, see para. CH62400 of HMRC's *Compliance Handbook* manual. For late submissions other than for new contractors, there is a minimum £300 applied to tax-geared penalties.

Interest can also be applied to CIS tax deducted but unpaid at the end of a tax year, or to CIS tax that should have been deducted and for which no reg. 9 order has been given. This is calculated by the DMB and is not eligible for tax relief.

9.4 Recent changes and concessions

The recent consultation on CIS did raise the issue of nil returns. It was agreed that from April 2015, no penalties are to be charged for nil returns and for the months prior to that date, the penalty may be appealed on the grounds of no payments having been made to subcontractors.

The current scheme allows contractors to advise HMRC for six months in advance, that no return will need to be made. This sits on the system until renewed or until a CIS payment is made (should the contractor's circumstances change in the six month period).

There is another concession that HMRC recognise. If a contractor has no payments to declare but forgets to submit the nil returns, and then notifies a six month "dormancy" period, HMRC will extend this period backwards to allow the contractor to be a nil-returner from the earliest date and will cancel the penalties.

For contractors that realise a return cannot be submitted on time, there is a facility that may allow a penalty notice not to be issued, or "inhibited". If HMRC are contacted ahead of the due date for the return, and the reason is given for the likely late submission of the return, then if this falls within the usual definition of a reasonable excuse then the penalty will not be raised. This is particularly helpful in that it avoids the need for an appeal, but it is also possible that by advising HMRC ahead of time of the problem, some merit will be given for taking heed of the requirement for compliance.

9.5   Appealing penalties

If it seems that a penalty has been raised incorrectly or that there has been what is considered to be a reasonable excuse, an appeal can be made to HMRC. This should be sent online or in writing within 30 days of the date of issue of the penalty notice. The grounds for the appeal should be included in the letter. Pursuance of the charge will be held back while the appeal is considered, but only as long as the return in question has been submitted.

HMRC will reply in respect of the appeal – if it is refused, an internal review can be requested. Should this review agree with the original decision, the options are to accept it or to refer the matter to the First-tier Tax Tribunal, with the option of a referral to the Upper Tribunal if unsuccessful. Again, the charge will not be pursued until the decision has been made at the Upper Tribunal or until the date for making appeals has expired.

As with making appeals against GPS revocation, all of the details of the charge should be reviewed. HMRC are also duty bound to issue the charge without undue delay.

Following the 2014 consultation, an online appeals service was established in 2015 and is the principal method of appeal from April 2016, but HMRC guidance at CISR 65100 still allows for written appeals.

Law: SI 2005/2045, reg. 46, 47

9.6   Mitigation of penalties

As can be seen from the analysis of test cases, the FTT has restricted power over penalties; those case outcomes tend to be yes or no regarding reasonable excuse.

If penalties have been incurred, the best method of damage limitation is to appeal to HMRC, who do have powers of mitigation. HMRC will review accounts, cash flow forecasts and details of personal income, expenditure, assets and liabilities in assessing the amount of outstanding penalties in proportion to what can be afforded.

The HMRC guidance refers to mitigation where they have made an error or delayed the issue of forms or notices. It also refers to mitigation such that enforcing the penalty would cause "genuine and absolute hardship".

Finally, consideration of the penalty should be given, in "other exceptional circumstances such as the CIS penalty or penalties being wholly disproportionate to the offence". Many FTT hearings have rebuffed claims of disproportionality, being outside their remit. There does not yet seem to have been an appeal against an HMRC officer incorrectly exercising discretion with regard to proportionality, though as mentioned in **Chapter 17**, sometimes the FTT will be flexible in their consideration of a reasonable excuse.

HMRC are obliged to investigate reported postal or severe weather problems should they contribute to a late submission. The guidance refers to the occurrence of one such instance, but with revised guidance should this recur.

9.7   Recent analysis

HMRC have categorised both the reasons for the issue of penalties and the excuses claimed by contractors, which are as follows:

Postage issues	30%
Online issues	22%
Inactivity period expired	13%
Ceased to trade	6%
Domestic issues	6%
Paper return not received	3%
Paper return not signed	3%
Copy return submitted	2%
Change of agent	1%
Other	14%

It is thought that the shift to mandatory online filing and the change regarding nil returns have eliminated many of these.

10. Materials

10.1 Introduction

Within CIS, if a subcontractor provides and charges for materials as part of the service to the contractor, the intention is for that proportion of the charge not to include a profit margin and for it to be excluded from any calculation of tax to be deducted. Suppliers of materials with no labour element are excluded entirely from any CIS reporting requirements. This includes delivery to site or business premises.

10.2 Who does this affect?

For subcontractors with gross payment status, this is not an issue. All that is paid to them is done so without any need for distinguishing what element is for materials, labour, expenses or profit.

For net paid labour-only subcontractors, the whole amount of any payments is subject to deduction, irrespective of any expenses incurred.

Those providing professional services, defined as architects and surveyors, are exempt from CIS in any event unless their remit extends to become that of developers. Any time spent by other subcontractors in trying to interpret exactly what is needed on site, may not be classed under this heading.

That leaves the net paid subcontractors whose services include the cost of materials and the provision of plant as well as labour. Those businesses need to show separately on their invoices (or applications), the part of the total that is subject to deduction and that which is not. But how do they arrive at that deduction-exempt proportion?

Some simply do not bother. They accept the deduction of tax on the whole payment as a savings scheme for SA tax, or offset it against PAYE/NI/CIS liabilities due. Such businesses may have a mixture of net-paid industry work and gross-paid domestic work, so deductions are less of an issue. However, given the cash flow difficulties of many businesses involved in construction, parking this money up to be set against a payment months in advance that may not even be payable, is not a viable option.

Therefore, for that business to minimise its tax deduction legitimately, or to make the correct calculation of the proportion of a charge that is not subject to tax deduction – which is classified for CIS as materials – how should that be calculated?

10.3   Definition of materials

If actual building materials are provided as part of the subcontractor's service to the contractor, then according to HMRC, the amount not subject to CIS deduction should be the actual cost of those materials to the subcontractor. But that rather naively assumes that the subcontractor provides – or has delivered to site – materials for which can be produced one or more invoices arriving at exactly the amount charged for.

That may indeed be the case if a particular shade of paint, or type of cladding or roofing material, has been specified by the end client. But for such things as plasterboard, carpet underlay or cabling, the subcontractor will buy these in large quantities, to be used in several projects. If the price of copper pipe goes up, should the subcontractor include the price of the stock held when the job was priced, or the cost when it was installed – if he can remember which was used in this particular job?

If some remnant stock from an earlier job is used, should that be charged at the unit cost per the invoice, or at nil given that the whole cost may have been recovered in that earlier job?

Hold that thought for a minute. What HMRC wish to avoid are abuses of the scheme by subcontractors, who may be tempted to inflate the cost of materials so as to reduce the tax deduction artificially. A plasterer's charge to a contractor should not include 90% for materials.

So as long as the materials element is "sensible", no consequences should arise. This has not prevented HMRC from raising some rather semantic arguments. Indeed, in CIS340 the responsibility is placed on the contractor.

It says, the contractor "can ask for evidence of the direct cost of materials" – without defining what is evidence. Without provision of this evidence, the contractor must make a fair estimate of the actual cost of the materials.

The guidance in CIS340 does not spell out what the contractor should do with this evidence. Presumably, as with the declaration of consideration of self-employment in the monthly CIS return authorisation, the contractor should satisfy himself that all is well. But how can that be proved to an inspector?

10.4   Policing of materials

CIS340 states that if the materials element "looks excessive", an explanation may be sought by HMRC. How can a tax inspector that has never worked in construction determine what is excessive?

If a subcontractor has taken too long for the work or has made errors that created costs for the contractor, should any deduction be made from the materials element or (more likely) the due-for-tax-deduction element? This often happens, so if the ratio shifts from 50:50 of materials/labour to 80:20 because of that reduction in authorised payment, is the HMRC inspector then going to penalise the contractor?

The best defence for the contractor in this situation would be to ask that the inspector proves that the tax and accounting treatment was reckless, and the evidence for arriving at that conclusion; also to ask how much tax was lost to Treasury as a consequence and to ask for a Regulation 9(5) finding (see **Chapter 14** for more details). Unless the materials were ludicrously overstated, it would be a brave inspector that took such a case to a Tax Tribunal.

HMRC have been quite assertive in this area recently. Contractors have been asked to evidence the deductions for materials, insofar as copies of invoices have been requested. Nowhere in CIS340 is it suggested that contractors should ask for this from their subcontractors. Whilst this might be a good idea (should this be practicable), it is just more time to be spent on compliance by the contractor. As mentioned in **Chapter 14**, this is something else in which HMRC can be asked to exercise their powers under Schedule 36 of FA 2008 – in other words, to ask the subcontractor to justify his figures but under the principle in CIS Manual 83050 that HMRC should not recover more tax than is correctly payable.

10.5 Other deductions to be included with materials

A subcontractor may include with materials, cost of plant hire. That is, actual costs charged by third parties for the provision of plant including fuel for its operation and presumably, though not stated, any costs for the delivery of that plant to site.

What may not be included is any charge for plant that the subcontractor owns. Therefore a net paid scaffolding firm must suffer full deduction of tax from its payments unless any poles or other equipment are hired in. HMRC make no recognition of the fact that scaffolding boards have a limited life and may not be repaired.

One complication that can be raised is when a plant hire company provides an operator with the item of plant. If the invoice simply specifies plant hire, then it can be regarded as such, not least because the hiring company is unlikely to be CIS registered and would be unhappy at having tax deducted. But what happens when the plant hire invoice indicates a labour charge as part of the overall cost? Is that merely a breakdown of the cost or is the company asking for tax to be deducted from that element of the cost? In CISR14240, there is a direct reference to plant hire with operator for use on site, as being an integral part of construction. Therefore the plant hire company needs to be verified, the whole of the cost should be processed by the contractor of that service through CIS, with the non-labour element treated as materials and the labour element subjected to tax unless the hirer has GPS.

Other than plant hire, that is it. All other costs sustained by the subcontractor must be met from the net sums received.

10.6 No recognition of materials

If a subcontractor invoices a contractor and shows – correctly – part of the charge as being for plant hire, the contractor may ignore this and apply the tax deduction to the whole of the payment. What should the subcontractor do?

As this pertains to an incorrect deduction, as covered in **Chapter 14**, the options are to accept the position and redeem the tax later, to ask the contractor to correct the deduction or to apply to HMRC with the details of the excessive deduction. The only difference here is that HMRC may refuse on the basis that the contractor has made what was felt to be a necessary correction. The time and effort to argue the point may not be worth the outcome.

10.7   Test cases

The contractor cannot simply contend that the materials element of an invoice looks correct and then insist that such satisfaction is its own evidence. This was the principal tool used in *Flemming*, to question an HMRC assessment based on excessive statement of materials; in the absence of any other evidence, the FTT upheld the assessment.

The issue of exemptions for travel expenses was not fully explored in *Refit Shopfitting Services*; on the face of it, these should not be exempt from deduction, but HMRC granted a reg. 9 direction. Claiming such a direction, as with failure to deduct tax from labour costs, should be a defence to negotiate with HMRC before going to FTT, especially if the subcontractor will co-operate.

Lack of knowledge of CIS, leading to the acceptance of material costs stated (as plant and other expenses) can be costly – the contractor lost heavily in *Doocey* in such a situation. This emphasises the need to ensure that staff dealing with CIS understand its complexities. This can occur in small contractor firms, or much larger companies such as *Maypine*.

It would be of benefit for accountants to talk to their construction clients about their procedures for invoice authorisation, to prevent such costs occurring.

Cases: *Refit Shopfitting Services v HMRC* [2012] UKFTT 42 (TC); *Flemming & Son Construction (West Midlands) v HMRC* [2012] UKFTT 205 (TC); *Doocey North East v HMRC* [2014] UKFTT 863 (TC); *Maypine Construction Ltd v HMRC* [2017] UKFTT 833 (TC)

11. Redemption of CIS deductions – individuals and partnerships

11.1 Partnerships

The tax that has been deducted by contractors under CIS is intended to be offset against other tax. CIS is not a tax in itself, merely intended to act as a hedge against loss to the Treasury and to be an acceleration of tax yield, in respect of sole traders and partnerships.

At the introduction to this book, it was stated that partnerships would be bracketed with sole traders for the purpose of ease of reference. That will be the case in this chapter, though with this early caveat.

Partnerships have their own UTR and have to be registered with HMRC for CIS. Therefore when a contractor makes a deduction of tax, it is against the partnership; the details of that business are entered in the contractor's monthly return and the deduction certificate shows the tax deducted from the partnership.

But the partnership does not have its own tax assessment. What happens to the tax deducted in respect of the partners' individual tax assessments?

When completing the partnership tax return, the final taxable profits are divided between the partners. However there is no provision on the return for the division of CIS deductions. Therefore, the answer is that the deductions should be shared between the partners in the same ratio as the profits.

The remainder of this chapter will refer only to self-employed individuals.

11.2 Basics of offsetting deductions

11.2.1 Self assessment and relevant periods

From the beginning of CIS, workers paying income tax and Class 4 NICs have claimed the deductions against their overall liabilities. There has been no offset against any other taxes throughout its existence, other than temporarily while repayments are agreed.

With regard to the redemption of CIS deductions, the time periods are different. The assessment for a tax year is usually based on the accounts for which the year end date falls between the respective 6 April to 5 April time period. For commencements, cessations or accounts of more than twelve months, adjustments to the taxable profits are made.

However, when redeeming CIS deductions, it is the sum of deductions for that tax year that is applied to the liability. It is incorrect to make any separate calculation by reference to the accounts.

In this respect, the subcontractor is beholden to the contractor. If the contractor declares that a deduction was made in the month ended 5 May instead of 5 April, the subbie has no choice but to accept it. This could delay the recouping of that tax by twelve months, but unfortunately those are the rules.

The subcontractor could appeal to the contractor for an adjustment. In practice, this is unlikely to happen, as by the time the payment is received, with or without the deduction statement, the contractor will have submitted the monthly CIS return (in that short 14 day window) and quite probably have signed off the RTI for that year as well.

The contractor will not want to unravel or amend all of this. In practice, the subcontractor is unlikely to ask for this, as obtaining payments from contractors can be difficult enough, as well as deduction statements – not to mention future work.

11.3   Deduction statements

11.3.1   General principles

Such problems aside, the subcontractor will collate the deduction statements relating to the tax year in question, total the sums deducted and apply that to the tax return and thereby the tax calculation. This assumes that there are no problems with doing this.

11.3.2   Missing statements

In practice, unfortunately, problems are all too common. HMRC's own survey found that one in five contractors do not issue deduction statements to all subcontractors, and one in three subcontractors claim not to receive them all. As mentioned in **Chapter 15**, HMRC have – after many years of ignoring their own responsibilities – begun to crack down on non-compliant contractors in this regard.

You find that there are some certificates missing. Either they were not issued or they have been mislaid. What do you do?

One of the benefits of the current scheme is that you do not have to send in the certificates to HMRC. Before August 1999, when all tax returns were on paper, the SC60 vouchers had to be sent in to obtain credit; after then, the CIS25 vouchers. This is not the case now; you simply apply the figure to the relevant box on the tax return.

In the simplest case, for example where £500 was invoiced and £400 paid, it may be safe to assume that £100 of tax was deducted under CIS. If you are non-VAT registered, there were no materials involved and you are unaware of any issues that may have given rise to a short payment – and if this is the only certificate missing – then you can probably add £100 to your list of certificated figures and make the claim.

You may be asking for trouble in any other situation.

Those outside the industry, including a lot of accountants and HMRC staff, are unaware that some net-paid subcontractors do not issue invoices for work done. Applications for payment are sent to the contractor, for the period in question (which may be specified in the contract), in which the subcontractor states the value of the work done, at the site in question – which may be as a single figure or as a percentage of the agreed contract sum. This may include costs for materials used or delivered to site. This is so VAT is not declared and paid far in advance of its receipt and to avoid endless corrections in subsequent returns. Most contractors self-bill for VAT, though a few request a VAT invoice when a payment is made.

11.3.3   *The difficulties in estimating deductions*

Let us say that a VAT-registered subcontractor applies for £10,000, of which £4,000 is for materials. If the contractor's QS disagrees with this, for whatever reason (all of which would fill another book), the payment may be authorised for £8,000, of which £3,000 refers to materials.

So £8,000 less 5% retention gives £7,600. From this, £950 CIS is deducted, calculated as follows:

£8,000 – £3,000 = £5,000
£5,000 x 95% = £4,750
£4,750 x 20% = £950

Deducting this from the £7,600 gives £6,650.

Adding VAT at 20% on the £7,600 (£1,520) produces a payment of £8,170.

Without the deduction certificate, it is impossible to interpolate how much tax under CIS has been deducted if all you have are the original application figures of £10,000 and the figure on the bank statement of £8,170.

This also assumes that the payment figure relates to something. The contractor's finance department may not have all of their systems computerised, and if they have, they may not work properly. The figure may be calculated on an incorrect premise. What is also a possibility is that a payment on account has been made, perhaps in response to desperate requests for payment, which may be a round sum. This can be formalised later, such that the correct payment is calculated and the on-account payment deducted; the entry on the CIS monthly return may not be until this later occasion.

You may disagree with the contractor regarding some of the reductions in payment. That is a business issue for you to resolve, but for CIS and your own tax affairs, you can only claim what has been declared and deducted to HMRC. You cannot make up the difference with the tax that you think you should have been deducted.

So, you are missing more than one deduction statement and you can only guess at how much tax has been deducted – and declared – from those payments received. What can you do?

11.3.4   Options available

You have two options. One is to guess the deduction figure, put it on the tax return and hope for the best. In calculating the risk of this strategy, you need to be aware of how the HMRC systems work.

What they do not have is a perfect massive spreadsheet of deductions, with contractors across the top and subcontractors down the side, categorising all deductions for the tax year agreeing to the RTI EPS figures at the bottom, and totals for all subbies on the right hand side, linked to the subbies' tax returns and designed for red lights to flash if a subbie claims the wrong figure.

Well, they have something like that, but it is not perfectly reconciled. HMRC can access deduction records by subcontractor UTR (albeit compromised for partnerships). This is not done regularly or systematically. So, however tempting it might be to enter a grossly overstated CIS deduction figure to claim a temporary repayment in order to ease cash flow pressures, this cannot be recommended.

If there is no possibility of obtaining the missing deduction statements, or if asking for them is a sensitive area, the information can be obtained from HMRC directly. For self-employed people, HMRC will provide the information, if in each case you specify the contractor, the dates and payments for which information is missing and what you have done about trying to obtain the information. It will take a few weeks for this information to arrive, so it is a good idea not to wait until after the end of the tax year unless you have no choice.

One thing to note is that it is now common practice, in the run up to 31 January, for HMRC to deploy a number of officers to check larger SA repayments.

Therefore, although HMRC can – and often do – make SA repayments in a matter of days, do not assume that your claimed amount will be in the bank next week. Some claims, even if completely legitimate, will be held back for scrutiny. It would not be a good idea to make a deliberately optimistic or overstated claim hoping it will go through on the nod, lost amongst thousands.

11.4   Insolvent contractors

What if the contractor has gone bust? In that case, the tax deducted from you but not paid to HMRC is HMRC's bad debt. If tax has been deducted from you but nothing sent in to HMRC, then what you need to do is to set out the applications or invoices issued, the sums received and what you consider to be the CIS tax deducted. It is recommended that these details are submitted with the tax return, explaining how the CIS deduction figure has been arrived at, and remember to declare that there are estimated figures in your return.

11.5   Gross payments

What if you receive payments without deduction of tax? That is the contractor's responsibility, not yours. The sum is treated as turnover, as usual; there is no deduction to reclaim, so it is simply the case that you have received the money rather than HMRC. The tax due will be the same. If the contractor subsequently has to pay the tax, this cannot be redeemed by the subcontractor.

11.6   Offsets against other liabilities

Referring back to the comment about offsetting repayments deriving from CIS deductions; they can only reduce or eliminate a liability under SA, but repayments that have been claimed and are as yet unpaid can be used as collateral with HMRC for other liabilities.

If money is tight and there is an impending PAYE liability, for example, then you can apply to HMRC to have the repayment recognised – just so long as you do it before the other liability is due. This is especially important for sole traders and partnerships with gross status, as there is no in-year offset against PAYE.

HMRC have been accommodating in this area in the last few years, though there is a limit to their leniency. If you have applied for Time to Pay arrangements in the past, due to shortage of funds, your application may be refused. If so, in such a case as this, point out that the shortage of funds is due to delays within HMRC. This should tip the balance in your favour. Remember to document such conversations, in case you need them for future GPS contentions.

See **16.4.11** for a discussion of test cases set out where problems occurred with set-offs, typically where the contractor simply assumed that the CIS credit would accommodate another tax liability.

11.7   Repayments during the tax year

The following applies to all subcontractors, irrespective of trading status. Although limited companies can offset deductions in-year against PAYE, there may be a recurring monthly surplus that has to wait until after the tax year, so an increase in that surplus may increase existing cash flow problems.

If deductions have been made incorrectly – at the higher rate, or at a time when the subcontractor held gross payment status – what are the options?

This can be left until after 5 April when the deduction is claimed as usual. If cash issues are such that the money is needed more urgently, the contractor can be asked to correct their return and make the payment. If the contractor is unwilling, an in-year request for repayment can be made to HMRC, sending in the details of the payment, the deduction certificate and the period when your nil or 20% deduction status existed. However, HMRC cannot make the repayment without a deduction certificate or without the monthly return having been submitted by the contractor and the respective tax paid.

Such repayments can only be made for periods after the date that the subcontractor registered for CIS. This process cannot be used to recover higher rate deductions if they were applicable at the time of payment.

If a subcontractor loses GPS which is then reinstated after appeal, this process cannot be used to recover tax deducted. This must be done in the usual way as, legally, the subcontractor had no entitlement to gross payment in the intervening period.

In the event of a deduction being made and queried by the subcontractor on the question of scope, in other words whether the work done falls within CIS, HMRC can be approached for a ruling. An incorrect deduction can be amended by the contractor; if that is not forthcoming, an in-year repayment can be made by HMRC to a sole trader or partnership, but only to a limited company subcontractor if cash flow difficulty can be proven due to the PAYE offset facility.

For subcontractors that cease to trade part-way through the tax year, an in-year repayment can now be made using form CIS40, introduced in April 2017. This can be submitted by post or online; applicants will be asked if the liabilities from previous years have been settled.

Law: SI 2005/2045, reg. 17

11.8 A cautionary tale

In what I hope is a coincidence, this happened to one of my own clients.

The 2015-16 SA return was prepared in accordance with the client's records and by reference to the CIS deduction certificates held (which tallied with the records of net income). The return was submitted online and the client received the repayment due. Six weeks later, HMRC demanded the money back.

HMRC claimed that the subcontractor's record on the CIS register did not disclose the deductions made. It was subsequently established that those deductions had been made, declared and paid over by the contractor concerned. HMRC have been unable to explain how this discrepancy occurred.

Furthermore, HMRC failed to follow their own procedures. The "amendment" to the tax return was made under TMA 1970, s. 9ZB and the letter to the taxpayer stated clearly that the matter was not that of an enquiry.

It was pointed out to the HMRC officer that in their own manual at CISR 74030, credit to the subcontractor for the deduction should be given *unless an enquiry has been opened*. Also, at CISR 75050, it states that "the only route however for allowing a deduction that is less than that claimed on the SA return is by opening a Section 9A enquiry".

An apology was issued and compensation paid to the taxpayer.

This may have been a one-off error. However, bear this in mind if HMRC repay less than is requested, and ensure that they follow their own procedures.

12. Redemption of CIS deductions – limited companies

12.1 History

In the early years of CIS, deductions made from the income of limited companies were redeemed against corporation tax, much as they continue to be for sole traders and income tax.

Companies in construction tend to be larger. There are not many individual subcontractors in the industry working through their own personal service companies, and the action taken against managed service companies in April 2007 reduced the individual-corporate tie up yet further.

The size of companies and the pressures on their cash flow, created by storing up deductions to be redeemed as many as 21 months later (when there may not even be any corporation tax liability), was recognised in 2002. The rules were changed such that companies could offset deductions suffered each month against PAYE, NI & CIS liabilities due to be paid.

12.2 Current system of offsets

That amended system remains in place. The contractor declares and pays the net sum, or pays nothing should the deductions be greater than the liability, keeping an aggregate total from month to month in the tax year. There are no checks by HMRC in the course of the tax year, unless the contractor happens to undergo a physical inspection of records.

For each month, this is how the offset works. The contractor totals the deductions of PAYE, employees' National Insurance, student loan repayments and CIS tax deducted from its own subcontractors; and adds to this employer's National Insurance, and adjusts for any SSP, SMP or SPP.

If that sum is greater than the CIS tax suffered by the contractor in that month, the net sum is paid to HMRC. If it is less, no payment is made and the monthly sums are rolled forward and aggregated until a payment is due or until the year end, whichever is sooner. HMRC have prepared a template, CIS132, as guidance for the month-to-month process.

The deduction of CIS tax suffered is declared through the RTI system, netted off when submitting the EPS return. If the contractor has no employees, there are no PAYE deductions but there is still a PAYE scheme in place and submissions are made in the same way, with the contractor recognised as XP in the HMRC system.

After April 5, any net sum due to the company can be reclaimed. However, this process is not as straightforward as for sole traders and partnerships. Even though the net sum due to the company was shown on the P35, now on the RTI FPS, there is no automatic repayment method established by HMRC.

It is necessary for the company to submit a formal claim to HMRC for the sum due, quoting the PAYE references, the respective liabilities and the deductions suffered.

Law: SI 2005/2045, reg. 56

12.3   Application problems

This process has been the cause of a lot of unhappiness both in the construction industry and the accountancy profession. A recap of the history of the process may help.

Up to 2009-10, claims by companies were submitted to their local district offices. As part of the move to close offices, to centralise processes and to make as much as possible online, for 2010-11 onwards all of the repayment claims were to be dealt with at Longbenton.

The impact of the economic downturn has given rise to increased levels of such claims. This was not fully recognised in the move to Longbenton; the effect was that companies were waiting several months for their repayments, even if there were no problems. Where the figures making up the claimed sum differed from the HMRC records, companies were asked for large amounts of information. The general approach was inconsistent and insufficiently co-ordinated.

There were many complaints to HMRC, with some companies desperate for cash resorting to lobbying their MPs to try and reclaim what was their money, being sat on by the government. The HMRC Longbenton team realised that the service had to improve.

There was a learning process to go through. Staff needed to realise that failure to receive a deduction statement was not actually the fault of the subcontractor. Too much time was being taken by staff trying to reconcile claims from information requested – because they lacked the necessary skills and because the information requested was not in a sufficiently concise format.

There had been insufficient analysis of the timing of claims, this information (if collated at all) having been spread across all the tax districts.

Having grasped the extent of the problem, HMRC provided a better service for the 2011-12 claims; still not great, but better. Hopes were high for a further improvement for 2012-13.

Which did not happen. There was no improvement at all, and still a lot of disappointment and discontent being expressed in industry and profession alike. This time, it seemed to be a matter of priorities. At the peak time for receipt of claims, staff were taken away from CIS repayments and put to work on administering tax credits.

The expression of discontent reached the highest levels of HMRC, and it was decided that Something Should Be Done. For the processing of claims for 2013-14, the target of payment within 25 working days was expressed. Anyone familiar with Orwell's *1984* and the Ministry of Truth may find parallels with the aim for 2012-13 of payment within 15 days.

12.4   Recent performance

How did HMRC perform with the 2013-14 claims? It seems as though the 25 day aim was met, though with the rider that where claims could not be agreed in full, part-payments and requests for information were sent out within that time. There are no overall statistics available, unlike in previous years; nor has there been any collaboration with professional bodies for the 2014-15 claim season, or any subsequent years. It would seem that HMRC are satisfied that nothing more needs to be done regarding procedures and performance.

Let us look at the process and see what may be done to make the claim easier.

12.5 Claiming a repayment

To begin with, a claim has to be made. That is something which many companies and quite a few accountants have yet to grasp.

The claim can be submitted as soon as is practical, even before April 5 but only as long as the final EPS and FPS have been submitted, which need to declare the deductions that have been made from the income of the company. Bear in mind, though, that HMRC need a couple of weeks to collate all of the information received from all contractors into an accessible format. Processing of repayment claims can begin from April 22.

This is one benefit from RTI – in the days of P35s, HMRC had to give contractors until May 19 for their submissions, so adding collation time and a bank holiday, June 5 was usually the earliest time that processing could begin. By which time there were sackfuls of claims, an ongoing mass of work that for 2012-13 only really came under control in October.

In June 2017, HMRC established the facility for online repayment claims. Helpfully, this allows for agents to make and administer the claim. However, if the repayment is to be made to that agent or a nominee, then a postal claim needs to be submitted. The information required is that for postal claims, as set out below.

If the claim is made by post, it can be on one page; quote the company PAYE references, the total liabilities due for the tax year, the total deductions suffered for the same period, the difference due to the company and something asking formally for the money, please.

Also give the bank account details, to which the repayment should be made. This is a real improvement made, after some lobbying of the DMB, from 2013-14. It used to be that all repayments were made by cheque – which added insult to injury to those desperate for the money, as they took a couple of weeks to produce, were sent second class, then took a further week to clear. HMRC – or more correctly, DMB – finally overcame their fears over the security issues of receiving bank account details from claimants.

At this stage, it is not recommended that you send in all of your deduction statements with spreadsheets showing how you arrived at your figures. Do not even send in copies. HMRC do not want this information at this stage, mainly because there is a good chance it will not be needed, but also because it has to be logged and then kept somewhere.

Send the claim to Longbenton, then wait. No, seriously. It is not a good idea to ring them up and ask how your claim is going. There are thousands of these in their office in the busy period of May to September, so it will not speed up the process and you may even lose your place in the queue.

What should happen next, whether the claim is made online or by post, is that, within 25 working days, a payment from HMRC appears in your bank account for exactly what you asked for. At the same time a written acknowledgement regarding the claim is issued by HMRC (with a cheque instead of a bank transfer if that was preferred).

That is, in an ideal world. Perhaps mostly ideal, because the HMRC officers do have an element of discretion in the processing of claims. If their records show a repayment due that is close to your claim, within their tolerance levels, then the higher of the two sums will be paid. That tolerance level is closely guarded, but it is not a percentage and is less than £500. This has been known to be flexible in times of claims backlogs.

From statistics of previous years, this will be the case for about 85% of claims. In fact, you may not receive a repayment if an offset has been requested; a significant proportion of approved claims are simply sent off within the HMRC system to clear liabilities (temporarily offset) for corporation tax, VAT or current PAYE. Also remember that the HMRC system will check for any unpaid liabilities or penalties – these will be deducted from the repayment.

12.6 Repayments on account

What if the difference in your claim and HMRC's figure is outside the tolerance level? It is not all bad news, and this is another recent improvement. The whole claim used to be held up pending resolution of differences, but now a payment on account can be issued (or offset against another liability). This, despite the DMB people claiming originally that this was not possible.

A cheque, or if you have provided the necessary details, a credit to your bank will arrive. But now comes the really tiresome part. The difference needs to be reconciled – you could simply cede the claim for that difference, but if an offset has been granted, HMRC are unlikely to allow that to sit there forever.

12.7 Reconciling differences

Let us say you want all of your money. What will HMRC ask for?

Ideally, they would send you copies of their records showing their figures, to agree with the payment on account, so you can cross-check these against your own records and establish how the difference has arisen. Unfortunately, they will not do that. Their legal advisers have said that this should not be done, for whatever reason – perhaps data protection. HMRC's own CIS people disagree with this and wish it were different, but it is not.

They will send you nothing useful, but ask you for information that is likely to take some time to put together. You will need a list of CIS deductions that correlates to the sum given in the original claim, drawn from the certificates (and any guesses you made). This list has to be cross-referenced to the certificates, and – you are not going to like this – to the company bank statements.

It has been pointed out to HMRC that companies do not always bank the cheques they receive, individually. So you are going to have to copy the paying-in slips as well as the bank statements. Then start work with the highlighter pen. Do all that you need to do, to prove to someone who is not an accountant that you have suffered the deductions claimed. Also consider whether the amount of the claim not paid is worth the extra work involved.

When that is done, bundle up the whole package and send it to Longbenton. Wait for a couple of weeks, then call them up. Keep pestering them until there is a resolution to your claim. As there is no 25 working day limit to processing difficult claims, HMRC staff can take as long as they like, or do as much as resources allow.

Eventually, the reasons for the difference will emerge. Most likely, a deduction was not returned or the contractor entered a different UTR on the monthly return, or the deduction was declared in the previous or following year. Amend the claims accordingly should there be an older repayment to claim.

In the case of missing deductions, query this initially with the contractor. If there is no co-operation, then an amendment to the accounts will be needed to correct for any tax deductions taken into account. That would be a compromise but at least some tax relief is gained on the shortfall.

If no contact can be made with the contractor, check with Companies House to see if the company has been dissolved or liquidated. In that case, a claim can be lodged with HMRC for the deemed tax deducted to be treated as having been paid.

In the event of payment being made without deduction by mistake by the contractor, there is nothing for the subcontractor to redeem, even if the contractor is ordered to pay the tax later.

Finally, it is not recommended that the director of a company should claim his company's CIS deductions in his own tax return to accelerate their redemption.

12.8   Top 10 tips

To try to reduce the problems occurring in repayment claims, after discussions with professional bodies, HMRC issued a list of the ten most common difficulties encountered, in the form of an advice checklist. This is a summary of that list:

1.   Ensure that the claimant's agent is authorised to act in making claims.
2.   Check that the subcontractor's name and UTR are correct in all documents.
3.   Check that all deduction statements are included with the claim and that they pertain to the correct tax year.
4.   If the business was incorporated during the tax year, check that the claim only relates to the company's deductions.
5.   Check that deductions have been made correctly and have been reported correctly on the monthly returns.

6. Check that the contractor has no outstanding monthly returns.
7. Check that the final EPS (or P35 if still outstanding) showing the deductions has already been submitted.
8. Check that all information requested by HMRC has been provided and within the timescale specified.
9. Verify how non-CIS overpayments have arisen when making the repayment claim.
10. If the business has ceased to trade, check that all monthly returns have been submitted.

12.9 Missing deduction statements

It was mentioned in **Chapter 11** how information may be obtained from HMRC should a deduction statement not have been received by a subcontractor. This applies also to limited company subcontractors, though there is an additional element that may be of benefit.

In s. 18(2)(a) of the *Commissioners for Revenue and Customs Act 2005*, disclosure of this information may be allowed if it "... is necessary for the carrying out of a function by HMRC. Necessary in this context means that there will be a direct benefit to the department for doing so, e.g. we carry out our functions more effectively".

It seems reasonable to interpret this as being a way that HMRC may reconcile a repayment claim difference and conclude the claim effectively. If the claim cannot be agreed in full at the first attempt, this should be quoted to HMRC as a request for any missing information. Especially as full access to information of CIS deduction is the main reason for the promised digital account.

12.10 Offsetting CIS repayments against other tax liabilities

This is mentioned in **11.6** above, but there is a greater incidence of problems with companies in construction, as they tend to be larger concerns.

It is possible for CIS repayments due, to be allowed to clear other tax liabilities such as VAT or corporation tax. However, it is not enough for the taxpayer to assume that HMRC's systems are all cross-referenced – a formal request for set-off must be made.

Current guidance says that this should be made in writing to HMRC, with the respective figures and references.

Failure to follow this procedure has proved costly for businesses. The outcomes of several cases are set out at **16.4.11**.

13. Self-employment and its interaction with CIS

13.1 Self-employment and construction

There is no such thing as a typical construction project. They are all unique – in fact, it may be better if they were not, because of the potential cost saving. Schools and hospitals could have a standardised, efficient layout depending on the capacity required, instead of the public sector wasting vast sums of taxpayers' money in trying to win design awards.

But that is to digress. The reason that the use of self-employed workers is so prevalent in construction is because there is far less certainty in forthcoming projects, in terms of their design and the mix of skills required, their location, size and time required. A business may have work for 1,000 people one month, and 400 the next. The intention was to need 1,000 for both months, but the second project was delayed. That's the dilemma; does a construction business employ all its workers, which keeps the good ones on board but exposes it to some serious risk of cost, or does it bring workers in as they are needed?

There is also the issue of downtime within stages of a project – a change in design, weather conditions, supply of materials, health & safety arguments, rare frogs on the site, unearthing ancient burial grounds – many reasons why the build can be held up. Productivity comes into it; it can be argued that employees are less productive because they know they will be paid – and the counter argument that employees work harder because they know they are better off, what with holiday pay and redundancy rights.

Interesting matters for consideration – if you want to read more, the report *The economic role of freelance workers in the construction industry* by Professor Andrew Burke, lately of Cranfield University but now at University College, Dublin, is well worth hunting out.

Construction businesses will always need temporary workers. They may be engaged directly as self-employed subcontractors or through agencies as self-employed or as employees, either of the agency or via an umbrella company. More about agencies later, but for now, let us consider subcontractors as self-employed. Well over a million subbies are CIS registered and in early 2014, around 800,000 would be active in the industry at any one time, a figure that has been used for many years and which is also borne out by the recent OTS report on self-employment. More than 1 million subbies had CIS deductions in 2016-17.

Indeed, the self-employed workforce is the very reason for CIS. If all subcontractors were paid gross, the additional layer of bureaucracy would serve no purpose. Therefore, the perceived risk to tax yield from the larger-than-average proportion of self-employed workers is why CIS was introduced in the first place and why it has been maintained for more than 40 years.

So how has this issue played throughout this time?

13.2 Genuinely self-employed?

HMRC have always raised the question of whether construction workers, treated as self-employed by their contractors, should instead be employees. Central to this approach is the idea that by being treated as self-employed, the worker avoids paying the "correct" amount of tax on his pay. In addition, the contractor avoids employer's NI – thereby gaining an unfair advantage in pricing for jobs (some would claim), by exploiting the worker and denying him employment rights (claim the trade unions).

The matter of self-employed status is dealt with most thoroughly by David Kirk; his book *Employment Status: The Tax Rules* (also published by Claritax Books) is highly recommended. For that reason, there is no need to condense the content of that publication here.

CIS has had some influence in this area. The requirement of a self-employed worker to register for CIS, whether that was with the Revenue initially, or to obtain a 714 and later a CIS4 or 6 card, has often been interpreted as the Revenue's approval of that worker's status, irrespective of the circumstances of the engagement: I am self-employed – this piece of paper/card says so.

Which, of course, would not always be the case. It did at least mean that the worker was paying some tax and offered the industry flexibility with its subcontractor engagements. That did not always satisfy HMRC, especially where the subbie worked for the same contractor year after year or where the 16 year old school leaver would become immediately self-employed, with (one would think) few skills and little practical experience to launch a business.

Such instances were discovered for the most part from PAYE inspections. HMRC also had a posse of trained status inspectors who would target potentially non-compliant businesses, of which those in construction were the most numerous.

HMRC did begin to take self-employment status more seriously from the late 1990s, in particular with the introduction of IR35 – aimed at limited companies, but with the status issues at its heart.

13.3   Employment Status Indicator

In the lead-up to 2007, HMRC spent a good deal of time and resources in developing the Employment Status Indicator (ESI). The intention was to give contractors guidance on whether a worker should be employed or self-employed given the circumstances of the engagement.

This was not designed solely to apply to the construction industry, but was generally geared that way as this was where it would be most regularly used.

The ESI is still in place today, with the same format of questions and sub-questions. In the current version, these cover the rights of substitution, control of the worker, financial risk and business structure.

In the early days of ESI, and indeed in the CIS manual guidance on self-employment, there was a significant element of cherry-picking those elements of court cases that suited HMRC. The bias inherent in the ESI design was pointed out and a slightly more balanced approach was taken.

There were also some inconsistencies, not least caused by the ESI being tweaked without any indication that this had taken place. Finally, in May 2007, version numbers were added but these have now been removed. One version stayed the same for four years; ESI in its original guise was updated in December 2014 and has been re-designed to accommodate IR35 queries from March 2017.

The ESI has held little credence in the accountancy profession. It has been used by contractors but again is compromised by HMRC's refusal to be held by its outcome.

How credible is ESI in its current format? The questions seem based on a paint-by-numbers approach, guided by the long list of cases of the last 50 years. That may not be a bad approach, but it loses something when the realities of construction come into play.

Substitution rarely comes into the equation and is becoming less credible as a defence. The control questions appear rather skewed. Financial risk ignores the question, what happens if the contractor goes bust? (The subcontractor is at the bottom of the list as an unsecured creditor.)

13.4 Testing the ESI

As a test, take the example of a self-employed scaffolder. Assume the worker is skilled and known to be reliable, which is why he has been working for a larger firm for some time; due to that firm losing out in the tendering process on a large housing development, he is now available. Let us assume there is another, smaller contractor that wishes to engage him.

Being a scaffolder, that worker will not provide his own equipment. Apart from it making sense to do so, the contractor will have its own poles, boards, ladders, barriers, plates and fitments because it is responsible for safety on site and cannot sign off on someone else's equipment. Doing so would also greatly increase its own insurance premiums, which are high for scaffolders anyway. Much as in the case of *Hall v Lorimer*, the worker is not being engaged to provide equipment, he is being engaged for his skills.

The contractor's latest site is local. The employees and the subcontracting worker can all get there by their own means. The contractor knows that the subcontractor will keep an eye on how the scaffolding is erected and put his own lads right if needs be, but will also own up to any of his own shortcomings and correct them himself. The subcontractor is engaged on a daily rate; quite a reasonable rate as the days are getting longer. The time limits of the project have been explained and agreed.

The contractor has other projects, another close to the first site. The subcontractor knows this and is aware that he might be needed there as well. It is barely two minutes' drive, so hardly a problem.

Working through the questions, substitution does not apply; the worker is a sole trader.

Under control, the worker is expected to know how to erect scaffolding in a safety-compliant manner. But the question asks, can the worker be told what to do? If it means interacting with the contractor's employees, yes he can; the contractor needs to decide who is to do what on the site.

Can he be moved from one task to another as priorities change? Yes he can, if additional equipment is required on the first site and the workforce can do nothing that afternoon, but the other site nearby could do with some extra help. The employees and the subcontractor take their own vehicles to that site, expecting to go straight home at the end of the day.

The following day, the subcontracting worker and one of the employees have to go to a third site; due to a mix-up with the contractor's suppliers, the additional equipment has not arrived, so they need to go to that other site which is being wound down – scaffolders call taking equipment down "striking" – to collect what is needed. As poles and boards cannot fit in the subcontractor's small hatchback or on the employee's moped, they collect and take the contractor's own flatbed lorry.

In the questions under the heading of control, therefore, the subcontracting worker can be told what to do (interaction), and moved from one task to another as priorities change. He is a skilled worker who knows from years of experience – and a recently attended course, which he needed to retain his CSCS card – what is needed, also the deadlines for the work.

Under financial risk, the subcontracting worker is paid a daily rate. He may work only seven hours if it rains heavily or there is a delay in equipment supply, but may also work ten hours to catch up or to fulfil the contractor's stated deadline – it is by being diligent in his work attitude that he is in demand. He pays his own expenses to go from one site to another. He is engaged as labour only, so equipment does not come into it. If the aforementioned ten hours are not enough, he will go back on the Saturday morning to finish up, having told the contractor – doing those extra couple of hours enhances his reputation, helps to ensure that payment will not be delayed and also gets him out of going round the supermarket with the wife and children.

He knows that payment could be delayed; it happened a few years ago with the same contractor when he went back on the Monday instead of the Saturday and charged for a full day. There was a heated exchange of views at the time, but the two men came to an agreement and there has been no trouble since.

The worker does not provide equipment, materials or a vehicle and is not paid for them, and in this engagement, no pay has been withheld.

The worker has only worked for one contractor in the last twelve months – though it is difficult to see how that should impact on this engagement.

The outcome of the ESI is that the worker is an employee. There is a low indication of substitution, but he cannot send anyone else. There is medium control over the worker, but that is often how construction work is undertaken, out of necessity – they do this, you do that and could you go down the road rather than waiting for something to arrive. There is medium indication of financial risk due to the lack of outlay by the worker, even though that is not why he is there.

Clearly, this is a ridiculous outcome produced by the ESI. It may have been less ridiculous had the question been asked about overseeing the contractor's employees, but this was not incorporated. A status inspector may also ask about the provision of the lorry, though there was no choice in this instance.

The control element makes no sense – at no time was this worker overseen. The financial risk – when the equipment did not arrive, if there had been no other site to go to, he would have been paid for half a day, but the employees for a whole day. He may not have worked at all the following day were it not have been for that third site being struck. He worked unpaid to complete work. The number of engagements he has had recently is irrelevant and has never been upheld in court as an employment clincher – HMRC's own guidance states that each engagement needs to be considered separately.

Again, this displays ignorance of working practices in construction by HMRC. For this reason, ESI cannot be recommended as a reliable tool for judging self-employment. At best, it is a partial checklist of the issues to consider.

The selective attitude to court and FTT decisions also seems to remain. Much as with a casino, the odds are in favour of the house. Much as with a casino, the ESI is probably best avoided.

Its credibility is undermined further by the parallel drawn from the IR35 forum. A series of business entity tests were drawn up over a long period of time (to determine whether a business existed or that the company intermediary was a sham), but towards the end of 2014, these were withdrawn. It was stated by HMRC that the tests had been little used.

The ESI was updated in March 2017, with its reach expanded to incorporate IR35 cases, with specific reference to off-payroll public sector workers. Many of those public sector bodies have found that workers with the skills needed do not want to be employed. Therefore the terms of the engagement are "clarified" to ensure that the worker is definitely in business on his or her own account.

The updating of the ESI does not appear to have improved it, with excessive weighting given to substitution and the provision of materials and equipment.

Case: *Hall v Lorimer* (1993) 66 TC 349

13.5   Declarations by contractors

When the current scheme was introduced in 2007, HMRC intended contractors to take the matter of self-employment much more seriously as well.

For the CIS monthly returns, then as now, the contractor must declare that "the employment status of each individual included in this return ... has been considered and payments have not been made under contracts of employment".

The intention was to raise the profile of status with contractors and the launch of the new scheme was considered to be the best time.

In addition, HMRC directors advised businesses that the number of status inspectors would be doubled. Some newly-trained staff were needed, following the *MAL Scaffolding* case of 2006, where HMRC inspectors were criticised for conducting an inspection with pre-conceived notions that the subcontractors were really employees.

Therefore, it made sense (and was more economic) for HMRC to raise yields by spreading caution. As it turned out, in the course of cost-cutting measures leading to older employees at the top of their pay grades taking early redundancy, the number of status inspectors has actually halved since 2007.

Some statistics from around this time demonstrate how the declaration may have had some effect:

2006-07

Reviews concluded	4,191
Cases where status incorrectly applied	748
Yield from status reviews	£17.2m

2007-08

Reviews concluded	7,262
Cases where status incorrectly applied	550
Yield from status reviews	£17.7m

However, the ESI was having very little effect, as can be seen from the decreasing number of times it was accessed by construction firms:

2007-08	access statistics, construction	38,000
04/08-08/09	access statistics, construction	8,300

Case: *Lewis (t/a MAL Scaffolding) v HMRC* (2006) SpC 527

13.6 Moving the goalposts

The issue of self-employment in construction remained and its profile was raised by the 2008 report *The Evasion Economy* written by Professor Mark Harvey of the University of Essex, sponsored by the union UCATT. This report, in common with earlier reports from the same source, claimed that there were 350,000 bogus self-employed workers in the construction industry. UCATT called for CIS to be scrapped and for workers to be employed.

Careful reading of this report reveals that the figure of 350,000 is little more than the borrowing of an equation from a study of construction in Germany, extrapolated for the UK.

Following this came the HMRC consultation document *False self-employment in construction* issued in July 2009. This document proposed that workers should be treated (or "deemed") as employees, unless they provided all of the plant and equipment required for the job, or all of the materials or other workers.

These proposals demonstrated an appalling lack of knowledge of the construction industry. Those involved in its drafting clearly had no idea how materials for a project are procured. The prospect of several bricklayers turning up with all of the bricks that they would individually lay, that would all be the same and that would be what the client wanted, is utterly unworkable and it was profoundly ignorant of those HMRC officers to assume so.

Contractors, whether they are landscaping, laying drains or cables, erecting a structure and playing whatever part in completing the envelope, will tender for the work based on material provisions and then obtain whatever they consider necessary to complete the task. This may involve 5,000 breeze blocks of a particular specification, but they may be bought in a batch of 20,000.

Similarly, plant will be provided from the contractors' own inventory or hired in. In both cases, the labour may be sourced entirely separately. It would seem that the case of *Hall v Lorimer* was either overlooked or treated as highly inconvenient.

To add insult to injury, under the proposals in the document, the worker would be subject to taxation as a worker but not entitled to any employee benefits.

The thought process appeared to be: employed good, self-employed bad. This took no account of the fact that, even back then, there were all manner of suspect umbrella schemes that would pay the worker a large proportion of their earnings as reimbursed expenses, leaving the remainder taxable with little paid to HMRC.

This document was severely criticised and degraded. The result was that in March 2010, HMRC agreed to shelve the proposals, blaming the economic downturn, but with a general warning of "just watch it" to the construction industry.

Those at HMRC who were particularly exercised about this, went quiet for the next three years, whilst trying to get the measure of the coalition government and coping with further reductions in manpower. The question was, what would be a valid reason to justify forcing thousands of workers into employment?

13.7   A new initiative

In the second half of 2013, the answer was found. Those dodgy umbrella/agency schemes seemed to be on the increase, with the ideas founded by that bent construction lot now spilling over into other industries such as delivery drivers and care workers.

The evidence for this was less than substantial. The same figure for bogus self-employed workers in construction, about 300,000, was trotted out again but this time cited as the number that were in disreputable expense-inflating schemes. This was less about the circumstances of the engagement but more about cutting the numbers of subbies.

There had been a crackdown on offshore intermediaries, for which the relevance and impact on construction was somewhat tangential, but this was a useful template. In December 2013, HMRC issued the consultation document *Onshore Intermediaries; False Self-Employment*, aimed squarely at the agencies that were particularly creative with definitions of expenses as well as guilty of "forcing" workers into self-employment.

Undoubtedly there have been such agencies, as well as those which treated the workers as self-employed without actually telling them. There are plenty of firms that offer high percentage levels of take-home pay of one's gross pay, and it does not take much time invested in research to establish that quite a lot of them have not been trading for long, in their current guise.

Their *modus operandi* is to offer the high percentage to workers who can scarcely understand the reasoning, even when explained, especially in the manner it would be explained. Perhaps those workers are a little too keen to be convinced.

There is also the issue of the agencies forcing workers into self-employment – there is work available, but under these terms. The higher pay, or at least the prospect of higher pay, acts as a sweetener for the loss of employment rights.

Those agencies deserved to have their practices questioned and to give credit to HMRC, the principal tool in this new legislation – this time – had an element of validity.

The crucial element of the engagement of a self-employed individual was whether he could work, and indeed did work, without "supervision, direction and control".

In one respect, this is fair enough. A worker such as the school leaver, or the person re-training or the worker capable of only basic labouring, can hardly be considered to be in business.

The downside of this is that many agencies have forced workers into employment. The new, untested law has spread caution and in many cases, unnecessarily. Skilled workers capable of earning upwards of £15 per hour are unlikely to require supervision, direction or control – though again, the circumstances of the engagement dictate the play as in one case a qualified locum doctor was held to be an employee.

The interpretation of those four words has become wider than needs be. Has he turned up? – supervision. Has he gone to the part of the site where the work is? – direction. Have his hours been signed off by the site manager? – control.

Some agencies have simply not bothered with the interpretation, and have put everyone on to PAYE or through an umbrella. The effects of this on the industry are already being seen, with the cost of employer's NI and the umbrella's fee eating into the worker's pay. The payslips provided are an interesting puzzle for a professional to solve, but almost impossible for the worker. Such workers may choose to look elsewhere for a living. Alternatively, if net pay is to remain the same, cost increases will be passed on to end clients. Of which HM Government is a significant player in the market, but of course such costs were not included in the impact assessment of the new legislation.

14. Failure to deduct – regulations 9 and 13

14.1 Introduction

Occasionally, a contractor will not have deducted tax under CIS from a subcontractor when it should have done so. This may occur from a misidentification of the subcontractor, a clerical error, a change in status, the contractor not realising that the activities fell within CIS or an overstatement of materials on the subcontractor's invoice – and this is not an exhaustive list.

This chapter covers the rules and options available in the *Income Tax (Construction Industry Scheme) Regulations* 2005.

Law: SI 2005/2045

14.2 HMRC's actions

Under reg. 13, HMRC must take steps to recover tax that has not been deducted, or has been under-deducted, by a contractor from a subcontractor once this has been discovered. A warning letter is issued to advise the contractor of the situation; this is to allow matters to be resolved at this early stage. If the contractor can recover the tax from the subcontractor, makes the payment and amends the monthly return, no further action needs to be taken. If the contractor can persuade HMRC that an error has been made in their analysis, such as an issue involving scope, the matter can also end there.

For businesses that find themselves to be deemed contractors for CIS, or where the contractor considers that there has been no tax lost from the non-deduction or where there is a lack of response or co-operation from the subcontractor, another facility is available.

Law: SI 2005/2045, reg. 13

14.3 Potential leniency

On the discovery, or voluntary declaration, of such an event, the HMRC officer has the option not to ask for the under-declared tax to be paid, subject to the matters set out in reg. 9. Penalties are a different issue.

Regulation 9(5) states that the HMRC officer *may* direct that the contractor is not liable to pay. With the emphasis on the word "may", rather than "must".

The circumstances under which HMRC may exercise discretion are set out in reg. 9(3). There are two conditions under which the tax would not be payable.

Condition A(a) is that the contractor satisfies the HMRC officer that he took reasonable care to comply with s. 61 of the Act and these regulations. Section 61 refers to the part in FA 2004 that governs deductions on account of tax from contract payments. In addition, under condition A(b), the contractor must also satisfy the HMRC officer that the failure to deduct was due to an error made in good faith or that he held a genuine belief that deductions did not apply to the payment.

Reasonable care is likely to vary depending on the contractor. A private person refurbishing a property to sell may be treated more leniently than the contractor operating in the industry, who is already operating CIS. The latter would have to demonstrate, for example, that the scope of the scheme was considered before making payment to a subcontractor for work that it turned out was within CIS.

A non-deducting contractor may appeal to the Tax Tribunal under reg. 9(7) should the HMRC officer not be satisfied.

There is another condition available, though this is not open to Tribunal appeal.

Condition B(a) is where the HMRC officer is satisfied that the subcontractor was not chargeable to income tax or corporation tax on those payments, or that the gross payments have been declared to HMRC with any due tax paid. Under condition B(b), the contractor needs to request the HMRC officer not to request payment under reg. 9(5), on the grounds that there has been no tax lost.

Therefore in response to the initial warning letter, it may be expedient to accept the situation that tax should have been deducted but to ask for an early consideration of the reg. 9 option. Which the HMRC officer is not obliged to do.

Law: FA 2004, s. 61; SI 2005/2045, reg. 9

14.4 What can the contractor do?

It is worth referring to the HMRC *CIS Reform Manual*, specifically paragraph 83050. This reiterates the content of condition B(a) and states the principle that HMRC "... should not recover more tax from both contractor and subcontractor than is correctly payable by the subcontractor".

Therefore the HMRC officer is obliged to check the compliance record of the subcontractor. The contractor must have the actual UTR of the subcontractor that was paid or some other true identifier. That check may show that all returns and tax are up to date, but of course the accounts figures submitted will in all likelihood include many other transactions. At this point, the HMRC officer may simply apply discretion and assume the gross payment has been included in those accounts; alternatively, enquiries may be made of the subcontractor.

To conclude the matter at this stage, a lot depends on the co-operation of the subcontractor. If he refuses to reply to the enquiries and it turns out that he has returned to his country of origin, the contractor is likely to have to pay up. Similarly if the subcontractor cannot be identified, for lack of a UTR being recorded, the liability will fall on the contractor and probably at the rate of 30%, so a gross payment of £700 produces an additional £300 of tax payable.

If the subcontractor is willing to co-operate and is fully tax compliant, then the HMRC officer should not issue any order for payment to the contractor.

There is another problem with which the contractor may have to contend, and that involves the time at which the gross payment was made and when enquiries are made as to the contractor's compliance.

For example, if a gross payment was made in April 2016 to a subcontractor with a 31 March 2017 year end, and the enquiry (and discovery) was made by the HMRC officer in July 2016, it could be

January 2018 before any return or tax payment – SA or CT – was made. That officer cannot be satisfied at the time of the enquiry, that the subcontractor has, or will have, made the requisite return or payment.

In those circumstances, it is difficult to see how the Tribunal could overturn a direction to pay based on condition B, so the options are to rely on condition A or to make a payment to HMRC. As there is no right of appeal under condition B, that tax paid is unlikely to be recovered.

There are two other options for the contractor in that circumstance. If the subcontractor is a limited company, then any CIS deductions would be offset against their own liabilities of PAYE, NI & CIS. If it can be demonstrated that the subcontractor has made the appropriate payment in full, which would otherwise have been net, then that seems to be reasonable grounds to ask the HMRC officer not to issue the payment direction.

Another is simply not to pay the tax, and wait until the subcontractor has submitted the accounts and paid any tax due, at which point the request can be made under condition B.

Again, this would require the co-operation of the subcontractor.

(With thanks to David Kirk, author of *Employment Status: The Tax Rules*, for identifying this anomaly.)

Finally, HMRC can be asked to invoke powers that they possess. In Schedule 36 of FA 2008, the second paragraph of Part 1 (Powers to obtain information and documents) states:

> "An officer of Revenue and Customs may by notice in writing require a person to provide information or to produce a document if the information or document is reasonably required by the officer for the purpose of checking the tax position of another person ... the taxpayer."

Therefore, in pursuance of the principle set out in the CIS Manual at 83050, that no more tax should be recovered than is correctly payable, it seems reasonable that a contractor in his defence should request HMRC to request information from the gross-paid subcontractor, to prove that such payments have been correctly declared.

If the tax has to be paid to HMRC, their guidance appears to be contradictory. CISR72080 indicates that the contractor's tax office should not allow an adjustment to the contractor's accounts to claim tax relief on the payment. However, at CISR82130, reg. 13 apparently allows a deduction for the payment in the profits of the contractor. Interest can also be levied (reg. 14), but this is not eligible for tax relief. Payments on account to HMRC from the contractor will be accepted to defray this interest.

Law: SI 2005/2045, reg. 9, 13, 14

14.5   Test cases

The correct identification of the subcontractor is important, as in the case of *Croftport* where it transpired that the subcontractor did not hold GPS. Given the verification system, this instance is unlikely to recur – the subcontractor was engaged initially before April 2007 – but it does emphasise the fact that the trading entity which has been verified should be the same as that which is being paid.

For proof of this, refer to *J&M Interiors*. A net paid subcontractor established two other companies which were paid net though only at 20%. HMRC raised an assessment to collect tax at 30% – though the contractor proved to the FTT that the payments had been made in good faith and was also able, with the co-operation of the subcontractor, to prove no loss of tax.

That co-operation is important, as was proved in *PVC Fascia*. Several subcontractors had been paid gross and reg. 9 was applied to a certain extent – but three subcontractors would not provide any details, landing the contractor with a tax payment of several thousand pounds.

Not making deductions on the basis that there was no need is unlikely to work as a defence. The son of a contractor's friend did some part-time labouring work; HMRC refused reg. 9, and despite the contractor providing evidence that no tax had been lost, the FTT still upheld the assessment on a punitive basis as the contractor was already operating CIS and failed to take necessary care with tax compliance.

Naivety will not be effective either. Accepting the promise from a subcontractor to declare income to HMRC if he was paid gross, proved to be a costly favour for the contractor in *Britannic Estates*.

Failing to recognise the need to operate the scheme properly proved costly in *Tayfield*. Their appeal against £79k of tax failed, for lack of knowledge of CIS – nil CIS returns were submitted, but in the belief that the company was a property developer and not a contractor.

It is always worth checking the circumstances of an engagement for technicalities. Two such exemptions emerged in *Buckingham* – the person organising workers was found to be a managing agent, not a contractor. Furthermore, the taxpayer held the properties in question as investments and therefore the workers' costs did not fall within CIS. Much the same conclusion was reached in *Donnithorne*.

Finally, an important principle was established in *PDF Electrical*. The office assistant verified the subcontractor but then entered the details incorrectly, making a gross payment. The FTT upheld the appeal after HMRC refused reg. 9, stating the following:

> "The standard required by Regulation 9 is that the business must take reasonable care in its compliance with the CIS. It does not require that mistakes must never be made."

This particular observation, given that it makes a specific reference to CIS, may be applied in other areas of contention with CIS. The findings in *PDF* also make reference to the difference between a substantial multi-national contractor and a small business in respect of reasonable care.

Reliance on the accountant has had mixed results, but this – combined with questions as to the scope of the scheme – helped *Mabe* in appealing against demands for £36k.

Law: FA 2004; SI 2005/2045

Cases: *Buckingham v HMRC* [2010] UKFTT 593 (TC); *PVC Fascia Company v HMRC* [2011] UKFTT 17 (TC); *Croftport v HMRC* [2011] UKFTT 419 (TC); *PDF Electrical v HMRC* [2012] UKFTT 708 (TC); *J&M Interiors (Scotland) Ltd v HMRC* [2014] UKFTT 183 (TC); *Britannic Estates v HMRC* [2014] UKFTT 974 (TC); *Tayfield Homes v HMRC* [2016] UKFTT 112 (TC); *Donnithorne v HMRC* [2016] UKFTT 241 (TC); *Mabe v HMRC* [2016] UKFTT 340 (TC)

15. Impact of the scheme

15.1 Introduction

Before 1999, the workings of the scheme were well established and well understood. Obtaining GPS was not difficult and the Revenue in general were sensible in reviewing tax compliance before making any revocations. Indeed, that was included in their guidance.

The retention of 714 vouchers and the maintenance of the SC60 deductions did add to the paperwork, but acceptance flowed from the residual guilt of the old days.

It is worth remembering that before the introduction of self-assessment in 1997, tax was assessed on the preceding year basis rather than the current year basis, and that thanks to estimated assessments, there was no great hurry to submit tax returns and certainly no £100 penalties. Interest and penalties were levied on late paid tax but there was less of a sense of urgency. No January 31 panics back then.

Tax compliance did speed up after then and, for the construction industry after August 1999, there was more to do and it had to be done more quickly than before. The industry did not like it, but the true extent of the additional burden was not really understood by those outside.

That changed with the report prepared by KPMG for HM Government entitled *Administrative Burdens – HMRC Measurement Project*, issued in March 2006. This looked at all areas of tax in which HMRC was involved.

15.2 Cost to industry of CIS

The report concluded that the administrative cost on all businesses for all taxes each year was £5.1 billion.

For those businesses operating CIS, the cost was £321 million.

That is 6% of the total. As the report found, "bearing in mind that this only applies to businesses operating in certain sectors, this is a fairly high proportion of the burden".

The report's authors could also have said, "unfairly high". The whole cost of administering VAT, across all businesses, only came to £1 billion. Proportionally, the cost of CIS is a massive amount for one industry to bear.

That figure of £321 million may have come as a surprise to HMRC. Whether it did or not, they chose to ignore it. In the Regulatory Impact Assessment (RIA) for the 2007 scheme, HMRC quoted figures of £52 million as the cost to the construction industry of CIS. Which figure – or source – would you find more credible?

That same RIA reckoned the reduced burden of the new scheme would bring the cost to the construction industry down to £30 million per year. Now, we know from the activity information available that in any one month at that time, there were 176,000 active contractors – as well as those that were inactive, but still needing to submit nil returns.

So, according to HMRC, on average every CIS contractor could cope with all of the demands of the scheme with half an hour per week of one person being paid minimum wage. That excluded any allowance for stationery, postage or internet costs.

Other than a grudging admission that the annual costs may exceed £100 million, no other references to the financial burden to the construction industry have been made since.

There were also the initial set-up costs for the new scheme. HMRC estimated these to be £40 million for all concerned. This was probably another underestimate, given that one FTSE 100 company – not in construction but with activities tangential to it – spent £1 million on new software to ensure CIS compliance. Losing GPS could be detrimental to the share price.

Returning to the KPMG report, after the largest single obligation of all tax compliance activity ranked by cost to industry (the issue of VAT invoices), the next three obligations were all to do with CIS.

The report also found that the burden of administration fell mostly on nano- or micro-businesses.

Regarding large companies, no publicly quoted company has ever lost GPS. The assumption is that there are sufficient people present to cover, check and review tax compliance that no such errors have ever occurred. Alternatively, it may be seen as additional circumstantial evidence of HMRC's preferential treatment of large business.

But for smaller businesses, CIS is yet another administrative task to add to all the others, except that losing GPS could have a severe impact on the business. Many examples of this as a plea to the courts are given in the next chapter, dealing with test cases, but for quite some time HMRC refused to acknowledge this.

The original HMRC figure for the costs of the current scheme of £30 million was clearly nonsense. An estimate of the annual cost to the construction industry is given in **Appendix 1**, to back up previous figures given by the ICAEW of £250-280 million.

15.3   Loss of gross payment status

In late 2005, and in a way due to the sharing of information on the internet, many more cases of loss of GPS were being reported. These are the rules, claimed HMRC, and the circumstances of each case were fought over.

Back then, some of the Revenue's tax offices had the resources to maintain detailed records of GPS reviews. The continued inconsistencies were revealed in a survey undertaken by the author at the time; one district declared a pass rate of 70% for new applicants and 85% for renewals – the one next to it geographically claimed a high of 97.3%. All other districts with specific figures had pass rates in between.

The harder line on GPS began earlier. In **Appendix 2**, the statement made in 1975 by the Board of Inland Revenue regarding tax certificates is reproduced in full. This was included in the Revenue booklet IR40(CIS), *Conditions for getting a subcontractors tax certificate*. At least, it was in the May 2001 version. It was excluded from the July 2003 version.

A few extracts make for interesting reading:

> "The Inland Revenue ... intend that the powers shall be used with discretion and common sense; and minor delays in submitting accounts or returns, or other instances of non-compliance which throw no suspicion on the general tax

reliability of a business, will not in themselves jeopardise entitlement to a certificate."

"The circumstances in which the issue of renewal of a certificate will be jeopardised are where the non-compliance has been so substantial, or of such seriousness, that it gives rise to reasonable doubt about the reliability of the business in relation to the way it handles its tax affairs ... ."

"Examples of non-compliance of this order include ... deliberate or reckless failure to meet normal obligations."

"Once issued, a certificate will be withdrawn during its period of validity only if there has been serious irregularity ... ."

That was the old way of thinking, so it must have been wrong. Except it seemed good enough for 26 years, and reading through the instances of non-compliance that cost businesses their GPS in the last ten years, it begs the question how many would have retained that status based on those earlier principles.

Alternatively, what was the risk to HM Treasury of many of those businesses retaining GPS? The findings of *Shaw v Vicky Construction* revealed too loose an interpretation by some of the General Commissioners, but the reaction seems to have been too far the other way. It was only with the *JP Whitter* case that impact on the business seems to have been properly considered.

Before that case, in 2008, a deposition of accountants met with HMRC staff to point out that businesses could be severely affected by loss of GPS as many contractors would not engage net-paid subcontractors. This went to minister level; the reply came back, "prove it". It was not clear whether that was a genuine request for evidence or whether it was given in the knowledge that it could be very difficult to prove; contractors tended not to make such clear distinctions in their invitations to tender.

By November 2008, HMRC had still only reviewed about 80% of all GPS contractors through their new centralised system (introduced in April 2007). The initial fail rate was 28%, decreasing after appeals to 14%. That would still represent about 15,000 contractors per year losing GPS.

111

From this point on, information was less readily available. The CIRIP review panel – now the Construction Industry Scheme Operational Forum (CISOF), was now meeting every third or fourth month, subsequently decelerated to every six months. Lack of HMRC resources meant fewer people to compile the information; suggestions of Freedom of Information enquiries were stonewalled as that only referred to information available, not raw uncompiled data.

Cases: *Shaw (HMRC) v Vicky Construction Ltd* [2002] EWHC 2659; *JP Whitter (Waterwell Engineers) Ltd v HMRC* [2012] UKFTT 278 (TC) and subsequent

15.4   Penalties

From April 2007, there was a bedding-in period of six months for the new scheme to allow businesses to become properly acquainted with the procedures. There were no repercussions for contractors that missed return dates within that period. Fewer cases of GPS revocation went through the courts at this time, but another problem for contractors began to build.

The new penalty regime started in October 2007; any of the first six monthly returns or payments that were still unsubmitted or unpaid after 19 October 2007 became liable. In its first 16 months, the HMRC computers issued a blizzard of penalty notices on the industry. Over two million notices were issued, for £217 million.

Many of these were issued to defunct businesses – that database problem again – or were raised incorrectly or successfully appealed. £83 million in such penalties were found to be incorrect.

By January 2009, only £10.5 million of penalties had been conceded and paid. Less than 5% of the total, but still a lot of money to come from one industry in just over a year for late submission of returns and late payments – this does not pertain to any tax lost to HM Treasury.

£123 million at that stage was rolled forward as collectible or pending the outcome of appeals. The new penalty regime helped to calm things down, but it is worth noting that in the HMRC 2012-13 Annual Report, £220 million of uncollected CIS penalties was written off.

Chapter 16 (test cases) includes many instances of unsuccessful appeals, often involving many thousands of pounds imposed on one contractor for basic non-compliance. In no other field of tax are such massive penalties levied except for deliberate tax evasion. As the First-tier Tax Tribunals often cite, that is the will of Parliament. How many MPs are actually aware of the existence of CIS?

15.5   An independent survey of the scheme

There were resources available for HMRC to commission a report from Ipsos MORI, titled *Evaluating the Construction Industry Scheme*, published in October 2010.

Some of the questions asked in the surveys are rather redundant; 52% of the respondents had no permanent employees and 62% acted only as a subcontractor. Asking these people how long they spent in administering CIS and whether it is easy or difficult (when they have only a handful of deductions in any year) is much less valid than when put to a contractor, and lumping the results together skews the results towards CIS being not very time-consuming.

That said, some useful statistics did emerge from the Report. The question "should CIS be abolished?" was not asked, but the answers to why there is a CIS showed that 36% thought it was to ensure that income tax gets paid. Tellingly, the next highest response was "don't know", with 32%.

Net paid subbies reckoned they received deduction statements from 67% of contractors. That is a lot of unissued statements. 80% of contractors said they provided statements to all subcontractors, which sounds inconsistent – more on that later.

Results on methods of payments were interesting; only 4% of subcontractors were paid by cash. Contractors said they made 7% of payments by cash. This puts paid to the perennial myth that there are large amounts of cash sloshing around the construction industry. It also asks a serious question as to the relevance of CIS.

Just as well for HMRC that the question was asked about businesses working in construction that deliberately avoided paying taxes – 5% said they thought this was very common, 22% said fairly common.

81% thought CIS was either very or fairly effective at ensuring such payment of tax.

Of the subcontractors surveyed, 9% said that they had lost GPS, but 61% had never had GPS. That makes it difficult to draw any conclusion as to overall percentages of revocation or denial.

There was one peculiar statistic; of those respondents that filed paper monthly returns, 21% said that HMRC did not send them partially completed forms. As HMRC insist that the figure is 100%, this perhaps compromises some of the responses.

15.6   Deduction statements – HMRC's failure to respond

It was apparent from a review of repayments of surplus CIS deductions to limited companies that there were problems in reconciling the respective records of HMRC and the subcontractors. This arose, in part, from the failure or refusal of contractors to issue the deduction statements, leaving the company subcontractors to estimate the tax suffered and later to try and prove that to the Longbenton claims department.

But as the Ipsos MORI survey revealed, a significant proportion of contractors were knowingly and admittedly not producing and issuing these statements. As there had been so much trouble with the CIS23/24/25 vouchers, this was left to the contractors to decide on the format (with some minimum of criteria) and was not built into the production of monthly returns.

Worse still, this report came out in October 2010. For over three years, HMRC had done nothing about overseeing this area of contractor responsibility, thereby neglecting their own responsibility to the net paid subcontractors. Following the report, nothing was done for a long time thereafter. Finally, after a lot of lobbying, reviewing statement issue became part of the procedures for CIS reviews (usually incorporated with PAYE & NI reviews) in 2014. Hopefully now the issue and receipt statistics will rise from the 80% and 67% quoted earlier. Whether the proposed digital online account for sub-contractors ever happens in the UK, remains to be seen.

But for all this time, HMRC did nothing to help the subcontractors; this was maybe not such an issue for the sole traders and partnerships, as they could estimate the tax deducted and enter it on the SA forms with no additional procedure for making claims. Only if the figures for CIS deduction were significantly out would this be investigated. Indeed, HMRC have reported few issues of fraud in this respect.

That said, many of the business proprietors and especially those with, dare it be said, non-professionals keeping the books of the business, are nervous of doing anything that may bring HMRC down on them, and in some instances will not have claimed back the tax deducted for lack of a certificate as proof.

The thousands of cases with repayments to limited companies that cannot be easily agreed are also handicapped by this procedure. This leads to what may be the greatest scandal involving the construction industry and CIS.

15.7   Unredeemed deductions

A Freedom of Information request revealed in late 2013 that massive amounts of tax are deducted from construction industry subcontractors, which are never redeemed against tax.

The total sum for the three years to 2009-10 came to just over £1 billion. HMRC have since confirmed that this sum continues to run at the annual level of £300-400 million. This is close to 10% of the total sum collected through CIS.

The reasons for this are not obvious. It is thought that some agencies or companies suffer the 20% deduction and choose not to submit any accounts, but under-declare VAT and PAYE, closing shortly after but then reappearing under a new name. Those suffering the 30% rate of deduction are likely candidates, but those subcontractors are a very small proportion of the total, little more than one percent.

HMRC promised to investigate the unredeemed deductions and have also been requested to look into ways of making the repayments. The investigation took more than 18 months to report back, having been provided with little resource or interest. The gist of the reply was that much of the difference was covered either with retrospective claims for deduction, or the tax that would have been payable from undeclared income of subcontractors.

It is worth speculating how much priority would have been given to investigating a £300 million shortfall in tax collection.

CIS was never intended to be a tax-generating scheme, but a method of more secure collection. That this has been known about and allowed to continue, represents another attack by HMRC on the construction industry.

15.8 Reining back

Prompted by ministerial meetings, HMRC were asked to consult with all interested parties and issued the paper *Improving the operation of the Construction Industry Scheme* in June 2014.

The minister's foreword stated the commitment "to making the tax system easier, quicker and simpler for businesses by reducing administrative burdens". It was left to HMRC to draw up the agenda for this consultation and they set about it with all the enthusiasm of a teenager clearing up his bedroom.

No opportunity was given for those interested to state their opposition to CIS or for alternatives to be considered. The questions put to consultation were within a very narrow field that was drawn up by, and acceptable to, HMRC.

The changes introduced from April 2015 are set out in **Chapter 18**. These do not represent any wholesale change or any significant reduction in administrative burdens. The greatest beneficiary of the consultation has been HMRC itself.

16. Test cases

16.1 Introduction

The decisions of the courts – and more recently, the tax tribunals – give a good indication of where the line is drawn in applying the rules of CIS to the many different circumstances.

In this chapter, the cases that apply principally to CIS are covered. The cases that refer to self-employment are well covered elsewhere. One or two cases of principle are included that have been applied to CIS cases, but only where mentioned in the discussion itself.

These cases have mostly occurred during the application of the current scheme. The rules can be seen to have changed and evolved since 2007. Cases before that date are included for useful background.

The cases brought mostly involve two areas of contention – over gross payment status and penalties. The "miscellaneous" section following that covers issues less frequently contended.

16.2 Gross payment status cases

16.2.1 Introduction

Given the potential impact on a business, it can often be well worth the cost in time and money for a contractor to dispute the decision of HMRC to revoke or refuse GPS – not that impact itself is an argument any more, following the *Whitter* decision in the Court of Appeal.

Since 2007, most cases have been brought by the contractor against HMRC. Before then, it tended to be the other way around. That is because HMRC decisions that were disputed were taken to the General Commissioners (GC). This was typically a board of three lay people, with a legal adviser, who would hear the arguments of both sides and reach a decision.

Quite a number of those decisions were based on common sense or an interpretation of the circumstances in relation to the outcome.

Where HMRC lost and it was felt that the legal principles had been left too far behind, the case was taken to court.

These are some of those cases. The name of the HMRC inspector is listed as the plaintiff.

16.2.2   Cases preceding April 2007

Vicky Construction Ltd – HMRC win

Despite a record of very little compliance in terms of paying tax on time, the GCs thought loss of GPS was too harsh and out of proportion to the failures. HMRC fought this on the basis that the continued non-compliance could not be regarded as minor and technical and, probably quite rightly, the court agreed.

Case: *Shaw (HMRC) v Vicky Construction Ltd* [2002] EWHC 2659

JDC Services Ltd – HMRC win

The contractor again had made many late payments of tax. However, the GCs thought that up to the date of the hearing, efforts had been made to bring all tax affairs up to date and that on that basis, and having been awarded large contracts, the contractor would be able to comply with all future tax obligations. This decision was thought to be legally flawed and the court overturned it. Whether the company lost the contracts as a consequence is not recorded.

Case: *Hudson (HMRC) v JDC Services Ltd* [2004] EWHC 602

Hilton Main Construction – HMRC win

Similar circumstances to *Hudson* above, though the contractor claimed the court had discretion to disagree with HMRC and also claimed that the disproportionality of the effect of loss of GPS was a breach of human rights. The court disagreed and this largely put paid to any other claims regarding human rights and GPS.

Case: *Barnes (HMRC) v Hilton Main Construction* [2005] EWHC 1355

Transform Shop Office & Bar Fitters Ltd – HMRC loss

Again, late payments – but the conclusion here was that because of their lack of action in pursuing or questioning the lateness of payments (back then, there was a three-year qualifying period),

HMRC acquiesced in this arrangement. Also, the court decided that as this had been brought to the contractor's attention, it did not necessarily follow that there would be future non-compliance.

Case: *Templeton (HMRC) v Transform Shop Office & Bar Fitters Ltd* [2005] EWHC 1558

CBL Cable Contractors Ltd – HMRC loss

Similar circumstances to *Templeton*, though with a let-off by HMRC on GPS in 1999. This came three weeks after *Templeton* but with no reference to it, by the different judge.

Case: *Cormack (HMRC) v CBL Cable Contractors Ltd* [2005] EWHC 1294

Lightpower Ltd 2005 ER 234 – HMRC win

More late payments but insufficient consideration by the GCs as to minor and technical.

Case: *Woods (HMRC) v Lightpower Ltd* [2005] ER 234

G-Con Ltd – HMRC win

HMRC had won this case in 2005, but the contractor appealed citing the decision in *Cormack*. The court reckoned the judge in *Cormack* had reached an incorrect decision and the appeal failed.

Case: *Arnold (HMRC) v G-Con Ltd* [2005] & [2006] EWCA Civ 829

Facilities and Maintenance Engineering Ltd (FAME) – HMRC win

The court weighed up all of the seven cases listed above in reviewing another case where the GCs allowed GPS for a late-paying contractor. The effect of loss of GPS was recognised, but reluctantly, the court had no option in law but to find for HMRC.

Case: *HMRC v Facilities and Maintenance Engineering Ltd (FAME)* [2006] EWHC 689

After the series of wins and the scepticism of the decision in *Cormack*, it all went rather quiet. There were a couple of cases involving the GPS of agencies and another that invoked human rights again, all being wins for HMRC.

The agency cases revealed some issues that were dealt with by the introduction of legislation taking action against managed service companies, on the same day as the new scheme began, 6 April 2007.

16.2.3   Cases after April 2007

The new scheme's method of reviewing compliance, coupled with the bedding-in period, produced fewer contended GPS decisions. The system of checking each company once a year took some time to initiate, meaning that those holding GPS held on to that status for a bit longer, perhaps allowing a few late payments to expire. Learning the rules of the new scheme helped contractors become more compliant, especially facing the new penalties.

The message sent to the GCs may also have hit home, i.e. stop being so lenient. This was also a time of serious downturn, especially in construction, so the Time to Pay arrangements – and the regular lack of cross-reference of those authorised late payments – may have helped out some GPS contractors.

In April 2009, the GCs bowed out and were replaced by the Tax Tribunals. The details and outcomes of these hearings are more accessible; these are some of the cases that dealt with GPS.

Grosvenor v HMRC – HMRC win

This is the first case arising from HMRC's internal review of a contractor's compliance. Tax had been paid late, the contractor had little in the way of reasonable excuse but appealed, unsuccessfully, on the grounds of impact on the business.

Case: *Grosvenor v HMRC* [2009] UKFTT 283 (TC)

Beard v HMRC – HMRC win

The economic downturn, causing late payments of tax, was the basis of the appeal. The contractor was unable to prove that bad debts and subsequent losses were the reason for the payments having been paid late, or that enough had been done to rectify the situation.

Case: *Beard v HMRC* [2009] UKFTT 284 (TC)

A Longworth & Sons Ltd v HMRC – HMRC win

Late tax payments had been made, in part arising from a change in the financiers of the business, but also due to a lack of awareness of the possible impact re GPS. This seems to have cost the contractor any sympathy from the FTT.

Case: *A Longworth & Sons Ltd v HMRC* [2009] UKFTT 286 (TC)

Mutch v HMRC – HMRC loss

The contractor was able to demonstrate how the rapid reduction of available work affected his cash flow, such that tax was paid late but as soon as possible. This was accepted as a reasonable excuse.

Case: *Mutch v HMRC* [2009] UKFTT 288 (TC)

Strongwork Construction v HMRC – HMRC win

The director of the contractor had broken his back, but the dates of the late tax payments predated the accident. This undermined the claim for reasonable excuse, also any claim for the loss of GPS being disproportionate was dismissed by reference to *Barnes v Hilton Main*.

Case: *Strongwork Construction v HMRC* [2009] UKFTT 292 (TC)

Munns v HMRC – HMRC win

Not so much late payments losing GPS as the fact that the contractor did not advise HMRC of his difficulties and agree a Time to Pay arrangement. *Barnes* again cancelled out claims re proportionality.

Case: *Munns v HMRC* [2009] UKFTT 290 (TC)

Ductaire Fabrication Ltd – HMRC win

Late paid corporation tax and a few late PAYE payments cost the company. No quarter from HMRC who cited *Grosvenor* (consequence of GPS cancellation not relevant) and *Transform* (strict compliance with tax obligations).

Case: *Ductaire Fabrication Ltd v HMRC* [2009] UKFTT 350 (TC)

Cormac Construction Ltd v HMRC – HMRC loss

A typical situation in construction; the husband does the work, the wife does the admin. There were some late payments and the mistaken idea that they were due by the 28th was not held to be a reasonable excuse. However, as the wife was balancing full time work and three children – one of whom was very ill after an accident – GPS was retained.

HMRC could have yielded on this case before the court hearing; their motivation seems to have been to put some definition on reasonable excuse. Another case was quoted in evidence, *Rowland v HMRC* 2006 (a dispute of a tax surcharge), such that a reasonable excuse "is a matter to be considered in the light of all the circumstances of the particular case".

Case: *Cormac Construction Ltd v HMRC* [2010] UKFTT 380 (TC)

Enderbey Properties Ltd v HMRC – HMRC win

Late payment arising from financial difficulties, but again, the contractor did not advise HMRC or seek any arrangement for payment – though such arrangements were made with creditors and suppliers. Proportionality again denied re *Barnes*.

An interesting point made by HMRC in their evidence: PAYE due to HMRC is deducted from employees' wages. A typical HMRC misconception, that employers start with a pot of money for wages. Also, employers' National Insurance is not a deduction. This was not contended in the case.

Case: *Enderbey Properties Ltd v HMRC* [2010] UKFTT 85 (TC)

Bruns (t/a TK Fabrications) v HMRC – HMRC loss

One late SA payment and a missing CIS return was the extent of the non-compliance. The contractor was 61 and unlikely to find employment, and loss of GPS jeopardised his business. It was also stated that sale of machinery would bring about severe economic loss.

It is difficult to judge how much the decision was influenced by nobody from HMRC turning up to the hearing.

Case: *Bruns (t/a TK Fabrications) v HMRC* [2010] UKFTT 58 (TC)

Bannister Combined Services v HMRC – HMRC loss

The partners had been in the habit of paying SA tax late. This was construed as acceptance by HMRC, but the FTT also appears to have been influenced by the late payments to the partnership, by local authorities outside of their obligations to pay within 30 days.

Case: *Bannister Combined Services v HMRC* [2010] UKFTT 158 (TC)

GC Ware Electrics v HMRC – HMRC win

The contractor had paid SA tax late and had been let off GPS revocation in 2008. The same thing happened in the next year, with the accountant being blamed for not advising the liability earlier. There does not seem to have been a strong play of the "reliance" card, despite the contractor working all over the UK. Loss of GPS derived from the contractor giving the obligation to make tax payments on time insufficient regard.

The court recorded the comment that revocation of GPS gave them no pleasure and that it appeared unfair, but legislation required such action. Little comfort for the contractor but an interesting shift in the tide of opinion.

Case: *GC Ware Electrics v HMRC* [2010] UKFTT 197 (TC)

Devon & Cornwall Surfacing Ltd v HMRC – HMRC loss

The contractors were entirely reliant on their company secretary to deal with tax compliance, but several submissions and payments were late. Holiday and sickness were cited as reasons but also, in correspondence, the HMRC inspector acknowledged that an unreliable broadband connection was partly to blame and that the contractor was expected to comply with future tax obligations. *Rowland* quoted again.

If HMRC were satisfied as to the contractor's future compliance, then it seems the purpose of the case was to extend the definition of reasonable excuse. Reliance on a trusted individual was confirmed, but also the broadband element. This is either a nod towards rural businesses or an implicit preference for online submissions.

Case: *Devon & Cornwall Surfacing Ltd v HMRC* [2010] UKFTT 199 (TC)

Getty v HMRC – HMRC win

Tax payments were made late, arising from a change in accountants but without the same practice of submitting pre-signed cheques (which the new accountant was unwilling to do). All the previously successful cases – *Cormac, Mutch, Radford* and *Bruns* – were cited, but the FTT held that the contractor should have paid more regard to compliance during the handover period.

This seems really harsh. Does this seriously suggest that the contractor would go on to be non-compliant?

Case: *Getty v HMRC* [2010] UKFTT 251 (TC)

Pollard v HMRC – HMRC win

Another reliance issue and another husband and wife scenario, except this time the husband was aware that his wife suffered from depression. Late payments were made and she was in the habit of hiding letters. This was determined as having insufficient regard to tax compliance.

Case: *Pollard v HMRC* [2010] UKFTT 269 (TC)

K1 Construction Ltd v HMRC – HMRC win

Late payments and submissions, no real excuse at all. *Enderbey* quoted in relation to *Barnes*.

Case: *K1 Construction Ltd v HMRC* [2010] UKFTT 347 (TC)

MR Harris Groundworks v HMRC – HMRC loss

All payments, including tax, were dealt with by an office manager and an assistant. Late payments were made; due to a lack of competence and arguments between the two, the manager was made redundant and the partners demonstrated a greater involvement in the financial issues of the business.

Mutch and *Rowland* were cited, but also another case, *Profile Security Systems v HMRC* (1996, STC 808) in which reliance was placed on "a trusted employee".

Case: *MR Harris Groundworks (a partnership) v HMRC* [2010] UKFTT 358 (TC)

Scofield v HMRC – HMRC loss

A serious analysis of the legal wording and HMRC procedures arose from a case where the contractor may have been expected to lose. There had been late payments. Cash flow difficulties were blamed but it was proved that funds were available to make the tax payment on time. No Time to Pay arrangements had been made.

What arose from this case, was that HMRC's own procedures were found to be inconsistent with the law. The automated review process, intended to streamline the observation of the tax compliance of over 100,000 GPS contractors as well as to achieve a consistent, non-localised series of outcomes, was found to be too automatic.

The court held that when the computer said no and the first warning of revocation letter was issued, no discretion by HMRC had been applied, as provided by FA 2004, s. 66, even though the contractor had a right of appeal upon receipt of the letter.

Following an adjournment for further argument on the meaning of section 66, the case was re-listed for the same Tribunal, with no change to the outcome. There was a weighty legal discussion as well as the revisiting of points in respect of impact on the business. HMRC's assertion that discretion was built into the computer program was rejected.

From this point, HMRC procedures had to change. We now have the procedure that the contractor is advised of any compliance failures that would mean revocation of GPS and invited to offer reasons for those failures such as may be regarded as a reasonable excuse. After that, the inspector makes a decision which the contractor may or may not accept.

Law: FA 2004, s. 66

Case: *Scofield v HMRC* [2010] UKFTT 377 (TC); [2011] UKFTT 199 (TC)

Glen Contract Services Ltd – HMRC win

Two notable points to take from this case; simply quoting cases is not enough, but also the FTT may not appreciate the difficulties some construction businesses have in receiving payment. The contractor had been let off GPS revocation in 2008, but again made late payments in 2009. *Mutch* and *Bruns* were cited, but there seemed to be a lack of firm evidence as to cash flow difficulties around the time of the late payments.

The court remarked that the financial difficulties resulted from the contractors' customers' reluctance to settle their accounts in good time. This was not regarded as unusual, as indeed it was not for thousands of businesses, just highly typical of larger businesses drawing finance from smaller businesses at a time when banks were avoiding risk, especially with the construction industry.

Case: *Glen Contract Services Ltd v HMRC* [2010] UKFTT 391 (TC)

RW Westworth Ltd v HMRC – HMRC loss

Another case where a consultant, well paid in this instance, was relied upon to run the finances of the business but made a series of late payments. This was regarded as a reasonable excuse.

Case: *RW Westworth Ltd v HMRC* [2010] UKFTT 477 (TC)

Williams v HMRC – HMRC win

Two late SA payments, each of less than £800 were the problem. Loss of business and cash flow difficulties were given as the reason, but though the business had an overdraft, it appeared that the contractor could have afforded to pay the tax on time. Not turning up to the hearing probably did him no favours.

Case: *Williams v HMRC* [2010] UKFTT 508 (TC)

Contrast that case with ...

Connaught Contracts (Bennett) v HMRC – HMRC loss

Though no cases were quoted by the appellant, evidence was given to the FTT to show why the SA tax had to be paid late, also that the partners had introduced almost all of their available personal funds to the business, which had suffered a significant reduction in turnover.

Case: *Connaught Contracts (Bennett) v HMRC* [2010] UKFTT 545 (TC)

Steve Jordan Fencing v HMRC – HMRC win

The FTT appears to have been unimpressed by the contractor's points that a cheque was sent but not received by HMRC and that his mother was later in charge of making payments.

Case: *Steve Jordan Fencing v HMRC* [2010] UKFTT 570 (TC)

S Morris Groundwork Ltd v HMRC – HMRC loss

The reason for late CT payment, being a delay in preparation of the accounts, was not regarded as a reasonable excuse but the effect of GPS revocation was. The FTT contrasted the findings in *Bruns* and *Grosvenor* and chose to side with *Bruns*.

Case: *S Morris Groundwork Ltd v HMRC* [2010] UKFTT 585 (TC)

Joseph-Lester (t/a Scaffold Access Services) v HMRC – HMRC loss

Several late payments, caused by a sudden loss of business. The contractor was able to demonstrate that with the need to maintain the business, payment of tax on time was not possible. The court agreed that this formed a reasonable excuse.

Case: *Joseph-Lester (t/a Scaffold Access Services) v HMRC* [2011] UKFTT 114 (TC)

Wright v HMRC 2011 – HMRC win

Confusion over tax liabilities from two businesses, whether claims to reduce tax payments derived from the contractor or the accountant and a general melee of who should have done what and when seems to have convinced the FTT that the contractor had an insufficient grasp of his obligations.

Case: *Wright v HMRC* [2011] UKFTT 824 (TC)

McDowall v HMRC – HMRC win

Time to Pay arrangements were not put in place until after the due date and the contractor had drawn significant sums from the business to help his son. Impact on the business was not supported by any cases quoted or evidence.

Case: *McDowall v HMRC* [2011] UKFTT 28 (TC)

Thames Valley Renovations v HMRC – HMRC loss

HMRC revoked GPS because the partners submitted their tax returns late, on the advice of the accountant as no tax was due. The court held it was reasonable to rely on the advice of a professional.

Case: *Thames Valley Renovations v HMRC* [2011] UKFTT 69 (TC)

Wood (t/a Propave) v HMRC – HMRC loss

The contractor applied his own Time to Pay arrangement to his tax liability without agreeing it with HMRC. This resulted in a late payment, but the FTT held that he had acted reasonably, also that they would have allowed GPS on the *Bruns* principle.

Case: *Wood (t/a Propave) v HMRC* [2011] UKFTT 136 (TC)

Ithell v HMRC – HMRC loss

The contractor made late payments, in one case due to an unsigned cheque. However, it was claimed that no notice was received of cancellation of GPS by the contractor or by the contractor's accountant. HMRC were unable to provide a copy of the notice to the FTT, which found that the burden of proof was on HMRC. No consideration of reasonable excuse was therefore necessary.

Case: *Ithell v HMRC* [2011] UKFTT 155 (TC)

Begbie (t/a Ready Steady Labourers) v HMRC – HMRC win

Late payments and returns, but little in the way of evidence or reason for this happening. No cases quoted in support of claim for impact on the business.

Case: *Begbie (t/a Ready Steady Labourers) v HMRC* [2011] UKFTT 184 (TC)

Kincaid (t/a AK Construction) v HMRC – HMRC loss

The contractor paid SA tax late, and only asked for a Time to Pay arrangement long after the due date. There was no representation for the contractor, on the grounds of cost, but the FTT appears to have treated this case sympathetically; on the basis that payments were made in accordance with the arrangement, this was regarded as good conduct and therefore GPS was retained.

Case: *Kincaid (t/a AK Construction) v HMRC* [2011] UKFTT 225 (TC)

Bruce (t/a Norrie Bruce Plant Hire) v HMRC – HMRC win

The contractor paid SA tax of £927 two months late. He appealed GPS revocation on the basis of delayed receipts but it later emerged that there was more than enough money in the bank account to cover the tax payment. The contractor admitted having been naive but then claimed reliance on advice. That, and arguments on proportionality and impact, were disregarded.

Case: *Bruce (t/a Norrie Bruce Plant Hire) v HMRC* [2011] UKFTT 241 (TC)

Industrial Contract Services Ltd v HMRC – HMRC win

Many of the cases above were cited in the discussion. The issue of HMRC's discretion was discussed in a case where £360 of Class 1A NIC was paid 20 days late. The contractor's problem was that only a year earlier, GPS had been retained after involving the local MP. Which you would think was the exercise of discretion, but this seems to have been one error too many, too soon.

Again, what risk is this contractor to HM Treasury?

Case: *Industrial Contract Services Ltd v HMRC* [2011] UKFTT 290 (TC)

Shaw Cleaning Services v HMRC – HMRC win

Late payments of SA tax and a late Time to Pay arrangement were the issues. Downturn in the industry, late receipts, impact on the business – all mentioned but not evidenced. Again, GPS had been retained in the previous year on appeal to the General Commissioners.

Case: *Shaw Cleaning Services v HMRC* [2011] UKFTT 378 (TC)

Duffy v HMRC – HMRC win

More late payments and claims of cash flow shortage which were unproven and undermined by some property purchases.

Case: *Duffy v HMRC* [2011] UKFTT 405 (TC)

McDermott v HMRC – HMRC win

And again – late SA payments, no particular reason.

Case: *McDermott v HMRC* [2011] UKFTT 477 (TC)

Cardiff Lift Company v HMRC – HMRC loss

A very involved case; several late PAYE payments, for which it was proved that timely payment would have exceeded the overdraft limit except for one. In respect of this, a partner's divorce and (unproven) illness in the office were disregarded and no reasonable excuse was found. But then the FTT discussed *Scofield* and found that no discretion had been applied, thereby voiding HMRC's decision.

Case: *Cardiff Lift Company v HMRC* [2011] UKFTT 628 (TC)

Piers Consulting v HMRC – HMRC loss

As above, late tax though caused by the bookkeeper. The FTT reserved judgment on that and held up the decision until after *Scofield* – and again, voided HMRC's decision for lack of discretion.

Case: *Piers Consulting v HMRC* [2011] UKFTT 613 (TC)

Forsyth v HMRC – HMRC win

An application for GPS was refused for late tax payments. These were attributed by the contractor to a bad debt, though this occurred some time after the due date for payment.

Case: *Forsyth v HMRC* [2012] UKFTT 209 (TC)

Dale Services Contracts Ltd v HMRC – HMRC win

The heart of this case is a late payment of CT of £333 but also the fact that CT due on 1 January was not met until the CIS repayment was agreed in the following March – no details are given as to why the repayment was agreed so long after the year end. Other matters were considered but rejected, with the following point worth remembering:

> "Reliance on a third party may be a reasonable excuse, but it is not necessarily a reasonable excuse ... relatively straightforward tasks which are delegated to an agent will not absolve the taxpayer if the agent fails to perform those tasks correctly."

Case: *Dale Services Contracts Ltd v HMRC* [2012] UKFTT 299 (TC)

East Midlands Contracting Ltd v HMRC – HMRC win

The contractor claimed that HMRC had not exercised discretion in withdrawing GPS, quoting *Scofield*. It emerged that HMRC had let the contractor off three times previously for late payments of tax, yet they still continued. No reasonable excuse was offered or found.

Case: *East Midlands Contracting Ltd v HMRC* [2013] UKFTT 25 (TC)

PSR Control Systems Ltd v HMRC – HMRC loss

The contractor had made one late PAYE payment. It was demonstrated at this time, there had been a bad debt, an overdraft application was pending and work was seasonal. A contract to supply a school needed to be agreed at much longer payment terms than usual. The FTT found that on their own, each of these was insufficient but that cumulatively, they constituted a reasonable excuse.

Case: *PSR Control Systems Ltd v HMRC* [2012] UKFTT 478 (TC)

Base Brickwork (a firm) v HMRC – HMRC win

There had been several late payments of SA and PAYE. The contractor demonstrated how its main client had unilaterally extended payment terms and that funds had been introduced to the business by re-mortgaging the partners' family homes. Unfortunately they represented to the FTT that they were unaware of the effect on GPS of paying tax late. Their contention that HMRC should have warned them was not accepted.

Case: *Base Brickwork (a firm) v HMRC* [2012] UKFTT 536 (TC)

JP Whitter (Waterwell Engineers) Ltd v HMRC – HMRC loss

This case had already been heard earlier in the year, which the contractor lost, but the company requested a relisting to set aside the decision. HMRC had already let off the contractor for late tax payments twice before. A lot of cases listed above were cited in the course of the hearing, but the findings came down to the financial impact. Finally, there was an acknowledgement by HMRC that loss of GPS would mean loss of business from larger contractors. Though this did not mean the end of the business, the FTT found that

HMRC's failure to take into account the financial effect of loss of GPS made their decision wrong in law.

Case: *JP Whitter (Waterwell Engineers) Ltd v HMRC* [2012] UKFTT 278 (TC) (and see appeals below)

John Kerr Roofing Contractors v HMRC – HMRC loss

One late payment of tax due to forgetfulness by the contractor brought about this case. After an extensive review of relevant cases, the court found that following *Whitter*, it had jurisdiction to review any decision made by HMRC in respect of GPS. As HMRC had, again, failed to take account of the financial impact, their decision was reversed.

Case: *John Kerr Roofing Contractors v HMRC* [2013] UKFTT 135 (TC)

Daniel v HMRC – HMRC loss

Some late PAYE payments when the contractor's daughter had died were conceded by HMRC as a reasonable excuse, but not the late SA payments. The financial problems of the business were regarded as unforeseeable. Also, HMRC had been asked for advice several times and had provided little of use. *Mutch* and *Joseph-Lester* were cited in the FTT for finding against HMRC.

Case: *Daniel v HMRC* [2013] UKFTT 136 (TC)

HMRC v JP Whitter – HMRC win

HMRC appealed the FTT decision to the Upper Tax Tribunal (UTT). The principal point of their argument was that in none of the legislation governing CIS, does it mention that the financial impact on a business has to be taken into account when revoking GPS.

The contractor's barrister made great play about human rights and proportionality, rejected by the UTT judges. The jurisdiction of the FTT and their original decision was also discussed.

The UTT upheld the appeal, and it was directed that the contractor should lose its GPS.

Case: *HMRC v JP Whitter (Waterwell Engineers) Ltd* [2015] UKUT 392 (TCC)

JP Whitter (Waterwell Engineers) Ltd v HMRC – HMRC win

With much at stake, the contractors took their case to the Court of Appeal. Retaining the same barrister, who made the same points, produced the same decision – GPS revocation was upheld. It was pointed out that the contractor should be aware of the consequences of loss of GPS and should have acted accordingly.

Case: *JP Whitter (Waterwell Engineers) Ltd v HMRC* [2016] EWCA Civ 1160

16.3   Penalties

Before beginning a chronological list of noteworthy cases, there is one recent case that deserves its own star billing.

Bosher v HMRC; HMRC v Bosher

Mr Bosher had made late submissions in the past and had settled up penalties levied up to 5 April 2007. Under the new scheme, there was further non-compliance and by the end of 2010, he had accumulated penalties of £54,100. HMRC offered to reduce these to £14,600, but the appeal was lodged. Following a long review of the issues, including proportionality, the judges rather strangely decided to undertake their own calculations, capping penalties at the amount of tax declared each month. They concluded that Mr Bosher should pay £6,287.

HMRC were not very keen on this idea, especially as they had pledged only to pursue £14,600, win or lose. The case came back to court where there was a long discussion of legal definitions, human rights and proportionality. The conclusion was that any mitigation should be with HMRC, that facility already being in place and that was sufficient recognition of human rights. Another point was raised regarding discretion, such that as with GPS in Scofield, the penalties should be void as they were automatically generated. The court did not agree with this, eventually finding for HMRC. It is not clear how much Mr Bosher eventually paid, but as the court concluded:

> "It is unimaginable that any court or tribunal would impose penalties of this amount for these defaults".

Cases: *Bosher v HMRC* [2012] UKFTT 631 (TC); *HMRC v Bosher* [2013] UKUT 579 (TCC)

SKG (London) Ltd v HMRC

The business incurred £2,800 of penalties for late CIS returns. These were disputed as being disproportionate. The FTT discussed this issue at length and drew parallels with a VAT case (*Greengate*) where there was no facility for mitigation, with which they were not comfortable. Before the case could be heard again, HMRC withdrew the penalties so no conclusion was ever drawn as to the proportionality of the penalties in these circumstances.

Case: *SKG (London) Ltd v HMRC* [2009] UKFTT 341 (TC); [2010] UKFTT 89 (TC)

Bells Mills Developments Ltd v HMRC

The company had engaged a much larger company with GPS to build residential properties. No tax was due and no CIS returns were submitted until the error was noticed. Some of the penalties were cancelled for the period when an accountant was in charge of the company's affairs, but upheld for the period after he had left.

Case: *Bells Mills Developments Ltd v HMRC* [2009] UKFTT 390 (TC)

Austin v HMRC

Mr Austin was dyslexic and trusted his accountant to deal with his CIS returns. Having changed accountants, it was found that no returns had been submitted, resulting in penalties of £15,100. The court found that Mr Austin should have made more effort to familiarise himself with CIS and to check on his old accountant. Penalties upheld in full.

Case: *Austin v HMRC* [2010] UKFTT 312 (TC)

Lewis v HMRC

The contractor paid the subcontractor gross "in good faith", later submitting the required returns. HMRC levied penalties of £38,400. *Barnes* was cited, but no proportionality could be applied. However, the FTT found that the penalties set out by Parliament had to stand, but that the additional penalties levied where the return was more than 12 months late, was open to FTT review. Those penalties, £25,200, were reduced to nil but £13,200 remained payable.

Case: *Lewis v HMRC* [2010] UKFTT 327 (TC)

Stone v HMRC

It is difficult to be sure which element of this case influenced the FTT more; Mr Stone's medical condition, requiring dialysis treatment, or that he registered for CIS (having operated the old scheme) but received no forms from HMRC for submission. HMRC contended that all other aspects of the business had been maintained, including VAT returns, but the FTT made great play of Mr Stone's efforts in earning an income from running a business. Penalties of £31,800 were set aside.

Case: *Stone v HMRC* [2010] UKFTT 414 (TC)

KD Ductworks Installations v HMRC

Inconsistent evidence seems to have cost the contractor the case; claims of non-receipt of forms and submitted forms being lost in the post. Two important matters arose; the fact that the appellant had no proof of postage, and the citing of *Stubbs v HMRC*:

> "These tribunals are a statutory creation and must apply the law as Parliament enacted it; fairness and equality are not matters they can take into consideration in arriving at their decisions."

Cases: *Stubbs v HMRC* (2007) SpC 638; *KD Ductworks Installations v HMRC* [2011] UKFTT 76 (TC)

Heronslea Ltd v HMRC

The contractor had been let off penalties before, but insisted as before that the return had been posted in good time by first class post – though it was not always possible or time-efficient to obtain proof. HMRC were unable to provide a copy of the date-stamped return, therefore the penalty was cancelled.

The same conclusion was arrived at, in the cases of *Gibson* and *Lilystone Homes*, the former supported by the respective payments having been made on time.

Cases: *Heronslea Ltd v HMRC* [2011] UKFTT 102 (TC); *Gibson v HMRC* 2011 UKFTT 113 (TC); *Lilystone Homes Ltd v HMRC* 2011 UKFTT 185 (TC)

135

Crooks v HMRC

The contractor registered late for CIS and incurred £1,500 of penalties. Ignorance of the law was no defence and Mr Crooks produced no evidence in support of the claim of the penalties being disproportionate. Penalties upheld.

Case: *Crooks v HMRC* [2011] UKFTT 246 (TC)

AJ Flack Ltd v HMRC

Again, late registration and £1,000 penalties. *SKG* was discussed at length along with other cases, but ultimately the case came down to reasonable excuse. Penalties upheld.

Case: *AJ Flack Ltd v HMRC* [2011] UKFTT 279 (TC)

Davies v HMRC

A late return with no proof of postage, with previous penalties having been cancelled. The FTT accepted the appellant's claim that the return and payment, though posted separately and to different addresses, were made at the same time and in time, proven by the presentation of the cheque. Penalty cancelled.

Case: *Davies v HMRC* [2011] UKFTT 303 (TC)

Castledale Building Services v HMRC

Many late returns and penalties of £36,100. The contractor claimed difficulties regarding a divorce, ill health and lack of funds, but provided no evidence to the FTT. He took over 15 months to discuss the matter with HMRC and still managed to run his business. Penalties upheld.

Case: *Castledale Building Services v HMRC* [2011] UKFTT 301 (TC)

Contour Business Interiors v HMRC

Several late returns and penalties of £1,500, attributed to a change in accountants. The court cancelled the first penalty, but not those subsequent.

Case: *Contour Business Interiors v HMRC* [2011] UKFTT 300 (TC)

M&J Plumbing v HMRC

Several late returns and penalties of £3,100. Proportionality and human rights claimed and dismissed – but with the new regime of penalties, HMRC applied those calculations to reduce the penalties to £1,900, which were upheld.

Case: *M&J Plumbing v HMRC* [2011] UKFTT 337 (TC)

Champion Scaffolding Ltd v HMRC

Several late returns and penalties of £7,600, reduced by HMRC initially to £5,000 then to £2,100. Reliance on the bookkeeper was claimed and *Devon & Cornwall Surfacing* cited – but the FTT rejected this for lack of supervision by the contractor. Reduced penalties upheld.

Case: *Champion Scaffolding Ltd v HMRC* [2011] UKFTT 375 (TC)

McGillen (t/a McGillen Building Services) v HMRC

A late return, following other quashed penalties. The contractor retained a dated copy of the return though no proof of postage. HMRC provided no dated evidence of their own. Penalty cancelled.

Case: *McGillen Building Services v HMRC* [2011] UKFTT 486 (TC)

Tony Bacon Decorators v HMRC

Just as above, but no mention of HMRC's evidence. Penalty upheld.

Case: *Tony Bacon Decorators v HMRC* [2011] UKFTT 497 (TC)

Scotts Glass and Glazing Services v HMRC

The contractor submitted photocopies of CIS returns. HMRC refused to accept them and levied £1,500 of penalties. The FTT cancelled the penalties, both for submission on time and holding that the format of the photocopies was exactly the same as the "approved" returns.

Case: *Scotts Glass and Glazing Services v HMRC* [2011] UKFTT 508 (TC)

PG Glazing Ltd v HMRC

Two late returns but payments made on time. No proof of postage, but no mention of HMRC's own evidence except that the court accepted that the HMRC system was a better system of receipt than that of the appellant. Penalties upheld.

Case: *PG Glazing Ltd v HMRC* [2011] UKFTT 562 (TC)

MEM Industrial Roofing Ltd v HMRC

Again, late return with no proof of postage; but held that HMRC cannot impose this as a requirement. Insufficient evidence presented by HMRC. Penalty cancelled.

Case: *MEM Industrial Roofing Ltd v HMRC* [2011] UKFTT 604 (TC)

Ireton v HMRC

Penalties levied for old CIS36 returns, of £2,400. Claims of lack of advice from accountant, delay in response from HMRC, change in address, human rights and proportionality all rejected. Penalties upheld.

Case: *Ireton v HMRC* [2011] UKFTT 639 (TC)

AE Joiners Ltd v HMRC

Late return, simply forgot. Penalty upheld.

Case: *AE Joiners Ltd v HMRC* [2011] UKFTT 672 (TC)

Regan v HMRC

Late returns, penalties previously cancelled, no proof of postage but no request for HMRC to prove date of receipt. Penalties upheld.

Case: *Regan v HMRC* [2012] UKFTT 21 (TC)

Koleychuk v HMRC

Many late returns, most of which were nil returns (after three months of contracting) and penalties of £10,000. Mr Koleychuk did not speak English well and often relied upon an interpreter. The FTT decided that the nil returns were not required and cancelled the penalties, upholding £1,000 relating to the three months of contracting activity.

Case: *Koleychuk v HMRC* [2012] UKFTT 224 (TC)

Project Developments (South Wales) Ltd v HMRC

Late returns and, initially, £8,200 of penalties. Some inconsistent evidence from the contractor, with claims of proportionality; dismissed by the FTT, but with an order to HMRC to re-calculate penalties due to the time taken to issue duplicate returns.

Case: *Project Developments (South Wales) Ltd v HMRC* [2012] UKFTT 322 (TC)

Westwood Houses Ltd v HMRC

A late nil return, but some contention over the penalty claiming it referred to £100 per 50 contractors. Court disagreed, confirmed penalties applied to nil returns, but reduced the penalty.

Case: *Westwood Houses Ltd v HMRC* [2012] UKFTT 166 (TC)

First in Service Ltd v HMRC

Return not received by HMRC. No proof of postage, HMRC's system accepted as satisfactory, and penalty upheld on balance of probabilities.

Case: *First in Service Ltd v HMRC* [2012] UKFTT 250 (TC)

Iles (t/a Purbeck Plumbing Heating & Drainage) v HMRC

Late return, blamed on the accountant – by the accountant. Several previous let-offs, penalty upheld.

Case: *Iles (t/a Purbeck Plumbing Heating & Drainage) v HMRC* [2012] UKFTT 389 (TC)

Masters At Carpentry Ltd v HMRC

Late online returns, apparently shown as "pending" on the screen – but inconsistent evidence from the contractor. Penalty upheld.

Case: *Masters At Carpentry Ltd v HMRC* [2012] UKFTT 510 (TC)

Dunn v HMRC

Late return in a previously advised nil return period, but the contractor waited too long (13th of the month) to request a form. Penalty upheld.

Case: *Dunn v HMRC* [2012] UKFTT 550 (TC)

Barletta (t/a Confurdec) v HMRC

Late return, taking 21 days to arrive, though contractor insisted it was posted in good time. No proof of postage. Penalty upheld.

Case: *Barletta (t/a Confurdec) v HMRC* [2014] UKFTT 382 (TC)

Savage (Savage Electrics Ltd) v HMRC

Late returns and penalties of £3,100. All correspondence was passed to the accountant unopened, so difficult to claim non-receipt of penalty notices. Failure of supervision. Penalties upheld.

Case: *Savage (Savage Electrics Ltd) v HMRC* [2014] UKFTT 521 (TC)

Mahal Construction Ltd v HMRC

An ill cousin and a son's wedding were not considered to be a reasonable excuse for late submission. Penalty upheld.

Case: *Mahal Construction Ltd v HMRC* [2014] UKFTT 530 (TC)

Woods v HMRC

Return two days late due to holiday. Penalty upheld.

Case: *Woods v HMRC* [2014] UKFTT 569 (TC)

Midlands Electrical Contractors Ltd v HMRC

Return one day late, previous penalties cancelled, human rights and proportionality dismissed. Penalty upheld. No mention of HMRC's evidence of receipt.

Case: *Midlands Electrical Contractors Ltd v HMRC* [2014] UKFTT 567 (TC)

Cunningham (t/a Cunningham Construction) v HMRC

Several late returns, penalties of £1,700 (reduced from £2,700). Contractor relied on the post but had no proof – and requested no evidence from HMRC. Penalties upheld.

Case: *Cunningham (t/a Cunningham Construction) v HMRC* [2014] UKFTT 566 (TC)

Oddy (t/a CMO Bird Proofing Specialists) v HMRC

Many late returns, but an insistence by the contractor that all were submitted on time and that reminders/penalty notices were not sent. The case involved a detailed review of HMRC's postal receipt system as well as their evidence, with the findings in *Heronslea* quoted extensively. Penalties of £3,700 cancelled.

Case: *Oddy (t/a CMO Bird Proofing Specialists) v HMRC* [2014] UKFTT 673 (TC)

Thomas Dalziel Steelfixing & Formwork v HMRC

Late returns, penalties which included those based on the tax deductions, total of £4,030. Long discussions over whether an appeal covers tax-based penalties as well as fixed penalties. Many difficult personal circumstances for the husband and wife, but also a lack of awareness re CIS. Court thought that reasonable excuse arising from special circumstances should allow for the penalties to be halved.

Case: *Thomas Dalziel Steelfixing & Formwork v HMRC* [2014] UKFTT 725 (TC)

Laithwaite v HMRC

The contractor relied on advice from his accountants on the running of the new scheme. Errors made resulted in penalties of £21,600, reduced by HMRC to £7,200. The FTT stated that though the penalties represented half his annual profits and therefore must be disproportionate, they had no jurisdiction to consider this, being a matter for the High Court. However, the FTT did as much as possible for the contractor, finding that there was reasonable excuse and also that the penalty had been incorrectly raised by HMRC.

Case: *Laithwaite v HMRC* [2014] UKFTT 759 (TC)

Daw Building & Plumbing Services v HMRC

Return allegedly posted on time, no proof of postage, no mention of *Heronslea* or request for HMRC evidence. Penalty upheld.

Case: *Daw Building & Plumbing Services v HMRC* [2014] UKFTT 759 (TC)

Miscellaneous cases where penalty upheld

Quite a few cases went through the courts around this time, which each contractor lost with the penalty upheld, under the following circumstances (which mostly involve a nil return one day late):

> *Expert Recruitment* – the contractor simply forgot
> *AGD Joiners Ltd* – poor broadband connection
> *Woodbine Electrical Ltd* – work duress and staff illness
> *Steyne Farm Co Ltd* – proprietors abroad
> *Elswood Mechanical Services* – accountant blamed
> *Viridian Energy Solutions Ltd* – "merely an oversight".

In the cases involving nil returns, HMRC pointed out that these could have been filed by telephone.

Cases: *Expert Recruitment v HMRC* [2014] UKFTT 738 (TC); *Daw Building & Plumbing Services v HMRC* [2014] UKFTT 739 (TC); *Viridian Energy Solutions Ltd v HMRC* [2014] UKFTT 785 (TC); *Elswood Mechanical Services v HMRC* [2014] UKFTT 786 (TC); *Steyne Farm Co Ltd v HMRC* [2014] UKFTT 787 (TC); *Woodbine Electrical Ltd v HMRC* [2014] UKFTT 789 (TC); *AGD Joiners Ltd v HMRC* [2014] UKFTT 790 (TC)

Turner v HMRC

Reliance by the contractor on an accountant who failed to act as required, but insufficient supervision of that agent; the contractor had operated CIS himself previously, so *Laithwaite* could not apply. Original penalties of £76,200 were reduced by HMRC on mitigation to £23,700 and later to £5,807. One point raised by the court – HMRC claimed the FTT had no jurisdiction as to proportionality of penalties, with which the judges disagreed, but not pursued due to the further reduction.

Case: *Turner v HMRC* [2014] UKFTT 1124 (TC)

Farrow v HMRC

This started as a reg. 9 case, but the main focus was on the £11,900 of penalties for late submitted returns. The case was stood over for *Bosher*, and after HMRC agreed to mitigate the penalties down to £3,376, these were upheld by the FTT.

Case: *Farrow v HMRC* [2015] UKFTT 28 (TC)

North v HMRC

The contractor was, by his own admittance, not very literate or knowledgeable of CIS. His wife prepared the returns, though she had suffered from MS for many years and had undergone treatment for cancer, though after the period in which returns were submitted late. HMRC mitigated penalties down from £31,500 to £9,000, which were upheld by the FTT for lack of special circumstances within the bounds of reasonable excuse. Consideration of financial hardship was a matter for HMRC within their powers of mitigation.

Case: *North v HMRC* [2015] UKFTT 56 (TC)

Okoro v HMRC

The appellant was registered as a subcontractor for CIS, but did not apply the scheme to other workers engaged for "a one-off situation", though one lasted for several months. The fact that the workers had declared their income to tax was not relevant, and (mitigated) penalties were upheld.

Case: *Okoro v HMRC* [2015] UKFTT 269 (TC)

CJS Eastern Ltd v HMRC

The owner of the business had operated CIS with full compliance. The advertising slogan from an agency "say goodbye to your CIS liability" seemed attractive, so he allowed the agency to take over the administration of the subcontractors. The agency were paid the sums requested each week, for more than three years until HMRC undertook a compliance check. It emerged that the sums paid were in fact net of CIS, which the contractor should have paid.

The unpaid tax of £14k was paid, but HMRC issued penalty notices for £81k, mitigated to £21k. The contractor appealed, claiming (amongst other issues) lack of proportionality, human rights and reliance on a third party.

Having considered *Bosher*, and revisiting the case, the judge was able to set aside £53k of discretionary penalties, but not the fixed penalties, for which proportionality could not be considered.

The moral of the story? If it sounds too good to be true, it probably is..

Case: *CJS Eastern Ltd v HMRC* [2015] UKFTT 213 (TC)

Merrin v HMRC

Penalties for late submission of CIS returns were mitigated from £144k (!) to £5.6k. The taxpayer appealed, through his accountant, citing human rights legislation and the delay in bringing the appeal to court. With some additional delay re *Bosher*, the case took over three years to come to FTT, which upheld the surcharge. The delay was held to have no bearing on the penalties levied.

Case: *Merrin v HMRC* [2016] UKFTT 240 (TC)

Barking Brickwork Contractors Ltd v HMRC

The company had administered its own CIS compliance, but then passed the provision of subcontractors to an agency. It submitted nil returns to HMRC, instead of declaring the payments to the agency (which had GPS). This was discovered in the course of a routine inspection and the company immediately submitted the 19 correct returns, though no tax was payable. HMRC claimed £12,700 of penalties.

Interesting evidence was obtained from HMRC, being the recording of telephone conversations. The first was from the company's bookkeeper, who rang to make a nil return and confirmed that no subcontractors had been paid. The bookkeeper left, and a second conversation took place between HMRC and the company owner's daughter, who was not an experienced bookkeeper.

The FTT held that HMRC did not provide the daughter with sufficient guidance and that there was a reasonable excuse for the non-compliance – the penalties were set aside.

Two useful matters arise from this case – firstly, the evidence of the telephone conversations, and remember that HMRC can destroy these records after a while. The other is an observation from the FTT judge, which is worth reproducing here in full:

> "Whilst we accept that there is a great deal of guidance available on HMRC's website and in its publications, it cannot be reasonably assumed that a taxpayer will have read all of it. Indeed, the very volume of the information makes it unlikely that even the most conscientious of taxpayers will have done so. Nor is it sufficient to say that a taxpayer should look for guidance on a particular matter, where, as here, the taxpayer reasonably believed that they were doing everything they needed to do and did not realise that any guidance was needed."

Case: *Barking Brickwork Contractors Ltd v HMRC* [2015] UKFTT 260 (TC)

MCM2 Cladding Systems Ltd v HMRC

Again, a case of the business owner relying on his bookkeeper (a qualified accountant) to maintain CIS compliance. Penalty notices kept arriving, so the FTT allowed reasonable excuse to apply to the point where the owner should have realised – by appropriate supervision – that all was not well. Proportionality dismissed, again.

Case: *MCM2 Cladding Systems Ltd v HMRC* [2015] UKFTT 254 (TC)

Gott v HMRC

Despite some difficult personal circumstances, the FTT held that the contractor was aware of the rules and should have submitted CIS returns on time. Penalties of £5,300 upheld.

Case: *Gott v HMRC* [2015] UKFTT 289 (TC)

Barrett v HMRC

There was a lot of legal discussion in this case, which involved two of my fellow Claritax Books authors, Keith Gordon and Ximena Montes Manzano; HMRC called Ken Claydon from their CIS team as a witness.

In brief, the contractor relied on his accountant for tax compliance, whilst under the impression that CIS only related to much larger businesses than his. The accountant did nothing for his client in respect of CIS.

The FTT held that the contractor had to pay £1,900 of tax that should have been deducted from one subcontractor (whose tax affairs were unclear), but that there was a reasonable excuse in respect of the penalties, which were set aside.

Case: *Barrett v HMRC* [2015] UKFTT 329 (TC)

Parkinson v HMRC

The contractor was a gardener and landscaper, who operated PAYE for several employees, but made payments to three workers. He was unaware that CIS applied and was fully compliant with all other taxes.

Penalties of £31,500 were mitigated down to £3k but the appeal still went ahead, including a claim of disproportionality. This latter was dismissed, but an element of reasonable excuse was accepted by the FTT judge, whose conclusion was that the penalties should be reduced to below £700.

Case: *Parkinson v HMRC* [2015] UKFTT 342 (TC)

Whitten v HMRC

Two brothers worked together, but the one who dealt with the paperwork fell ill. Some CIS submissions were not made. From penalties of £3,000, £1300 were dismissed as being out of time, but the others were upheld.

Case: *Whitten v HMRC* [2016] UKFTT 490 (TC)

B&I Plastering v HMRC

Even though the partnership had been submitting CIS returns, there was a period of over three years where no returns were made. The partners had left this to the bookkeeper, and the accountants were only involved in PAYE for the business.

The case was held over post-*Bosher*. Claims for proportionality and human rights were dismissed, and penalties of £33,800 were upheld.

Case: *B&I Plastering v HMRC* [2016] UKFTT 587 (TC)

Sowinski v HMRC

The taxpayer had relied on the advice of his accountant in respect of CIS. The accountant had attended a training course and gained the impression that CIS did not apply to businesses with a turnover of less than £1M.

The taxpayer had lived in the UK for many years, having moved from Poland, but the FTT accepted the representation that his English was insufficient to understand technical tax guidance.

Tax assessed under reg. 9 was dismissed, but the penalties of £5,700 were upheld, given the point at which the taxpayer should have questioned the advice from the accountant following letters from HMRC.

Case: *Sowinski v HMRC* [2015] UKFTT 636 (TC)

Crossman v HMRC

This case involved failure to register and submit returns and a failure to deduct tax. The contractor undertook domestic work but used other workers, and some of these were deemed to be employees. His (qualified) accountants did not pick up on the payments made and the CIS failure was only recognised when the contractor changed accountants.

The FTT asked both parties to reconsider their calculations, in light of evidence being obtained regarding the subcontractors' declarations, but also in how HMRC had calculated capped penalties.

Case: *Crossman v HMRC [2016] UKFTT 4 (TC)*

Alpine Contract Service Ltd v HMRC

The contractors were typically in a repayment situation, being subcontractors to larger firms. Therefore they did not submit nil CIS returns, nor returns where the company was due a repayment. HMRC raised penalties, which even mitigated came to £15k.

No tax had been lost, but HMRC pursued the case of potential loss of revenue. One of the company directors made the mistake of saying that they had been "too busy" to submit the returns. The FTT agreed that this constituted a deliberate action and dismissed the appeal.

Case: *Alpine Contract Service Ltd v HMRC [2016] UKFTT 394 (TC)*

PM Reinforcements Ltd v HMRC

Partial success for the appellant, in that evidence was produced that conflicted with that of HMRC in terms of CIS submissions. HMRC were directed to explain this, it being "important for the integrity of the system". Where the appellant could produce such evidence in support of the appeal, benefit of the doubt was given and penalties were reduced.

Case: *PM Reinforcements Ltd v HMRC [2017] UKFTT 434 (TC)*

ASM (Refurbishments & Decorators) Ltd v HMRC

Another person who was too busy was Mr. Dodd, who won a very big contract at the same time as becoming the main carer for his elderly mother. Tax compliance slipped and HMRC pursued £10k of penalties; these were upheld as Mr. Dodd had failed to meet his accountant on many occasions as arranged and had put no other procedures in place.

Case: *ASM (Refurbishments & Decorators) Ltd v HMRC* [2016] UKFTT 822 (TC)

Scott Building Contracts Ltd v HMRC

However, the cumulative effect of circumstances involving a new-born baby, a burglary, depression and an elusive accountant was enough to convince the FTT to allow an appeal against penalties for late CIS returns.

Case: *Scott Building Contracts Ltd v HMRC* [2017] UKFTT 630 (TC)

Dobbs v HMRC

Late registration for CIS was attributed by the appellant to a host of personal circumstances, as well as to reliance on his accountant. The FTT was not convinced and upheld the capped penalties of £3,000.

Case: *Dobbs v HMRC* [2017] UKFTT 163 (TC)

Other cases

Penalties were upheld where the appellants were simply late in registering or making submissions, with no reasonable excuse and no account taken of proportionality.

Cases: *Hills Painting & Decorating Ltd v HMRC* [2017] UKFTT 249 (TC); *Caunter v HMRC* [2017] UKFTT 335 (TC); *LC Property Management Ltd v HMRC* [2017] UKFTT 511 (TC); *Bolger v HMRC* [2017] UKFTT 627 (TC)

16.4   Miscellaneous

These are some other cases that do not fall exactly within the above two categories.

16.4.1   Investment properties

John Buckingham had investment properties, but was also occupied full-time in another industry. His son Matthew was between jobs so John asked him to look after the properties, paying him a weekly sum. Matthew engaged workers to refurbish the properties but paid them gross. HMRC held that Matthew was a contractor and assessed him for uncollected tax.

The FTT held that Matthew was a managing agent and therefore not either a mainstream or deemed contractor. Similarly John held investment properties and expenses did not fall within CIS. The assessments were dismissed.

Case: *Buckingham v HMRC* [2010] UKFTT 593 (TC)

16.4.2   Regulation 9 denial

In *PVC Fascia Company,* no tax had been deducted from subcontractors. HMRC initially assessed £20,133, but the contractor claimed under reg. 9 that it was not responsible for that tax.

After a review of tax records, it was found that three subcontractors were unwilling to co-operate; the contractor claimed that the gross income would have been declared and tax paid, but could not produce any evidence. The FTT found for HMRC in that for those subcontractors, £8,455 was payable by the contractor.

Case: *PVC Fascia Company v HMRC* [2011] UKFTT 17 (TC)

Tayfield Homes had registered for CIS, but submitted nil returns because it was thought that, as property developers, they did not need to deduct tax from their principal contractor.

The FTT found a very low level of diligence in the company as to CIS and refused the appeal against the payment of £79k of tax that should have been deducted.

Case: *Tayfield Homes v HMRC* [2016] UKFTT 112 (TC)

16.4.3   Reconciliation of accounts and CIS income

HMRC queried the taxpayer's income in *Devine* and found that the true turnover was greater than that shown on CIS deduction certificates. No convincing explanation was given for the additional sums banked and the taxpayer was assessed for the undeclared income.

Case: *Devine v HMRC* [2011] UKFTT 404 (TC)

HMRC opened an enquiry into Mr. Gjoci's tax return, which included nearly £9k of CIS deductions. Amongst many other unsubstantiated claims, it emerged that only £500 had been deducted through CIS for the year in question.

Case: *Gjoci v HMRC* [2016] UKFTT 576 (TC)

16.4.4 Failure to verify

The contractor in *Croftport* engaged the subcontractor before 6 April 2007 and paid gross on the basis of a CIS6 certificate seen. It emerged that the subcontractor had never held GPS and HMRC assessed tax of almost £18,000 plus 10% penalties.

The FTT held that the contractor genuinely believed the sub-contractor had GPS and thus did not make any verification. Assessments and penalties dismissed.

Case: *Croftport v HMRC* [2011] UKFTT 419 (TC)

16.4.5 Verifying deductions for materials

In *Flemming & Son*, HMRC questioned the amounts deducted for materials, in making net of tax payments to subcontractors. The contractor's main defence was that the regulations had been followed, in that the contractor has to be satisfied that the deductions represent the direct cost of the materials. No requirements were laid down as to how the contractor should obtain that satisfaction.

HMRC contended that this could simply be an agreement between contractor and subcontractor, but that it needed to be shown how the materials element was derived. Not surprisingly, in the absence of any other evidence, the FTT found for HMRC and agreed the assessment of £32,923.

Case: *Flemming & Son Construction (West Midlands) Ltd v HMRC* [2012] UKFTT 205 (TC)

Maypine Construction had an annual turnover of £25M and was operating CIS, but an inspection of their records by HMRC found that no adjustments had been made for subcontractors including travel expenses and use of their own plant in the non-deductible element of their invoices.

Appeals based on no benefit to the company, and acting in good faith were dismissed in favour of HMRC's argument that more care should have been taken, especially by a company in such a position. Tax payments of £21k were upheld.

Case: *Maypine Construction Ltd v HMRC* [2017] UKFTT 833 (TC)

16.4.6   Failure to deduct

The contractor in *Hoskins* failed to make tax deductions from a friend's son who did odd jobs and part-time labouring. No other subcontractors were engaged at the time and the assumption in good faith was that the worker would declare the income to tax. HMRC assessed the contractor for the tax due to be deducted and refused to make a reg. 9 direction. The contractor produced a statement from the worker, that tax had been paid on the income, therefore the assessment was double taxation.

The FTT found that the contractor, being well versed in CIS, had not taken sufficient care in his tax compliance responsibilities and upheld the assessments.

Case: *Hoskins v HMRC* [2012] UKFTT 284 (TC)

16.4.7   Honest mistake

In *PDF Electrical*, the contractor's admin assistant verified a subcontractor but mistakenly entered into the accounting system, GPS rather than pay net of tax. This came to light in an HMRC compliance visit – no tax was lost but HMRC refused to apply reg. 9.

The FTT held the contractor did take reasonable care and allowed the appeal, stating that a business should take reasonable care under reg. 9, but that it does not require that mistakes should never be made.

Case: *PDF Electrical Ltd v HMRC* [2012] UKFTT 708 (TC)

16.4.8   Classification of materials

The contractor in *Refit Shopfitting*, when making tax deductions from subcontractors, exempted from deduction sums given as travel expenses. This was based on previous experience from working for larger construction firms as a self-employed individual. HMRC refused to make a reg. 9 direction and raised assessments for non-deducted tax plus penalties.

In the course of the contractor's appeal, "new evidence" had been produced, though without any description of what that was. The FTT agreed that the reg. 9 direction should be made and the penalty set aside.

Conspiracy theorists may care to consider whether HMRC preferred that non-compliance by blue-chip construction firms should not come to light.

Case: *Refit Shopfitting Services Ltd v HMRC* [2012] UKFTT 42 (TC)

16.4.9   Overseas entities

The *Island Contract Management* case concerned an attempt to pay UK construction workers gross. ICM was an Isle of Man company which set up ICM(UK) and obtained GPS for that company from HMRC. The chain of payments was: the end client paid an agency for work carried out in the UK; the agency paid ICM (UK); ICM (UK) paid ICM; ICM paid the workers.

On the grounds that the workers had been paid by a non-UK company that was outside of the scope of CIS, it was argued that deductions were not necessary. The FTT held that ICM (UK) should have deducted tax from payments to ICM. It revoked its GPS and upheld assessments for non-deducted tax.

The company took the case to the Upper Tribunal, which upheld the original decision without qualification.

Case: *Island Contract Management (UK) Ltd v HMRC* [2012] UKFTT 207 (TC), [2015] UKUT 472 (TCC)

No deliberate error was found in *Schotten*; the UK company engaged, as its sole subcontractor, a company based in Germany. There was no verification sought for the company nor tax deducted. The directors considered that a non-UK company would not fall within CIS.

The tax that should have been deducted was £395k, for which HMRC granted relief under reg. 9(5), but sought penalties of £28k.

The appellant argued that this was one error, compounded over four years and not recognised as such by the accountant they had engaged throughout this period.

The FTT found that the appellants did have reasonable excuse and set aside the penalties.

Case: *Schotten and Hansen (UK) Ltd v HMRC* [2017] UKFTT 191 (TC)

16.4.10 Timing of deductions and human rights

The contractor in *O'Kane* generated profits in one tax year that gave rise to a tax liability; but having accrued debtors in calculating that profit, the tax deducted from the payments made by those debtors was not recorded until the following tax year. A surcharge was levied for late payment of the earlier year's liability.

The FTT held that the contractor had a reasonable excuse in believing that the tax deducted for the work would cover the liability and cancelled the surcharge. This decision was made due to the lack of available power of the FTT to cancel the surcharge, but by reference to human rights precedents the Tribunal was able to justify the disagreement with HMRC's position. Upholding reasonable excuse was the only available way to support the taxpayer.

Case: *O'Kane v HMRC* [2013] UKFTT 307 (TC)

16.4.11 Offset of CIS deductions

The issue of offsets occurs with regularity in contentions over VAT surcharges. These cases give some guidance as to the correct procedures to be undertaken.

The work of the business in *Graffiti Busters* was outside the scope of CIS, but clients had incorrectly deducted tax from payments made. The company was unable to pay its VAT liability and was assessed to a surcharge as HMRC refused to repay the CIS tax until after the end of the tax year, after offsetting PAYE.

The FTT agreed with the taxpayer and reduced the surcharge to relate to the amount not covered by the incorrect deduction.

Case: *Graffiti Busters Ltd v HMRC* [2014] UKFTT 61 (TC)

Another VAT surcharge in *French Polish*, levied on a company that was within CIS. VAT due in July was not paid until September when the refund of excess CIS deductions was made by HMRC. No offset was requested by the contractor.

The FTT held that the contractor cannot unilaterally apply set-off and upheld the surcharge.

Case: *French Polish Ltd v HMRC* [2014] UKFTT 91 (TC)

Cash flow was a continuing issue for MPH Joinery Ltd, in the appeal against VAT surcharges of some £15k. The appeal was dismissed because the company failed to demonstrate that the particular cash flow difficulties could not have been foreseen, and for the failure to make a formal request for set-off and time to pay.

Case: *MPH Joinery Ltd v HMRC* [2015] UKFTT 106 (TC)

Much the same occurred in *UPR Services*, where no request for set-off was made, though with a host of excuses for late payment. Surcharge upheld.

Case: *UPR Services Ltd v HMRC* [2015] UKFTT 415 (TC)

The Tribunal judge came down very hard on the appellants in *Quality Asbestos*, citing the amount and clarity of advice in the public domain in respect of CIS. Again, the lack of a formal set-off request – plus the figure quoted for CIS repayment that became rather less when finally agreed – cost the company dearly. Surcharge upheld.

Case: *Quality Asbestos Services Ltd v HMRC* [2015] UKFTT 595 (TC)

The timing of CIS repayments was different in *GH Preston Partnership*, but again the lack of a formal request for set-off counted against the appellant. The loss of GPS two years before the first default was not thought to be a reasonable excuse.

Case: *GH Preston Partnership v HMRC* [2016] UKFTT 296 (TC)

There was some success for the appellant in *SOS Joinery*, in that errors made by HMRC and the delay in their rectification were taken into account, whereby a reduction of the surcharge was ordered. An earlier case was also cited as being influential, though not binding.

Cases: *Paul Raymond Marsh v HMRC* [2007] UKVAT V20091; *SOS Joinery Ltd v HMRC* [2016] UKFTT 535 (TC)

There was no such success for the appellant that cited the difficulty of not being able to offset CIS repayments in-year against VAT liabilities, especially when combined with a late-paying client. Surcharges of £48k upheld.

Case: *East Midlands Contracting Ltd v HMRC* [2017] UKFTT 526 (TC)

16.4.12 Subcontractor identification

The contractor in *J&M Interiors* had been paying the subcontractor for many years, under deduction of tax. The (self-employed) subcontractor formed two limited companies but did not make it clear to the contractor that receipts would be processed through these companies. HMRC contended that as the companies had not been verified, tax of 30% should have been deducted.

The FTT held that the payments had been made in good faith and all the subcontractor's tax had been paid so no additional tax needed to be paid.

There was also some discussion in this case whether suspended ceilings came within the scope of CIS. It was agreed that they did.

Case: *J&M Interiors (Scotland) Ltd v HMRC* [2014] UKFTT 183 (TC)

16.4.13 Lack of CIS knowledge

The contractors in *Doocey* did not deduct tax from a subcontractor on some occasions where the invoice charged for plant or other expenses. The proprietors and the office staff were not well versed on CIS and thought deductions should only apply to labour costs. HMRC raised an assessment for the additional tax that should have been deducted. The FTT held that due to lack of reasonable care, the assessment should stand.

The summary of proceedings contains no indication whether the subcontractor defaulted on his tax liabilities. Rather surprising given that the assessment was for over £27,000.

Case: *Doocey North East Ltd v HMRC* [2014] UKFTT 863 (TC)

The owner of Thompson Heating left all tax compliance to his bookkeeper, who was unaware that having registered for CIS, nil returns and payments to subcontractors with GPS needed to be declared. Penalties were appealed on this basis, and also on the grounds of proportionality. HMRC's view was that this should be rejected and FTT upheld this, dismissing the appeal.

Case: *Thompson Heating (2000) Ltd v HMRC* [2016] UKFTT 165 (TC)

By contrast, Mabe appointed a chartered accountant who failed to spot that fire protection work could be covered by CIS. Even though Mabe was aware of the scheme and had suffered CIS deductions in the past, the FTT considered that he had taken reasonable care and the Tribunal upheld the appeal against £36k of tax demanded.

Case: *Mabe v HMRC* [2016] UKFTT 340 (TC)

16.4.14 Lack of CIS application

The contractor in *Britannic Estates* verified two subcontractors as net paid at 20%, but paid them gross on the promise that they would pay the tax due. HMRC contended that the tax had not been paid.

The FTT held that the gross payments had not been made in good faith, so no reasonable care had been taken. The Tribunal upheld the assessments for tax not deducted.

Case: *Britannic Estates Ltd v HMRC* [2014] UKFTT 974 (TC)

16.4.15 Trading activity or investment

It is not a CIS case, but there are some interesting matters discussed in the case of *Terrace Hill*. A property was held at FTT to have been an investment; this may help in rebutting claims of trade by HMRC.

Case: *Terrace Hill (Berkeley) Ltd v HMRC* [2015] UKFTT 75 (TC)

16.4.16 Subcontractor paid net or gross?

HMRC opened an enquiry into two of Mr McEwen's tax returns, querying the tax deducted under CIS, for which there appeared to be no evidence.

The facts emerged that he had been paid cash, on the basis that 20% tax had been deducted, but no deduction statements had been provided. The contractor's accountant that made the payments and had assisted McEwen with his tax returns, had since died. The contractor's records made no mention of McEwen at all.

It turned out that McEwen had grossed up the – apparently – net payments to arrive at the tax deducted under CIS. The FTT recommended that the figure actually paid to McEwen should be his gross income for tax purposes.

Case: *McEwen v HMRC* [2015] UKFTT 528 (TC)

16.4.17 *The accidental contractor*

Mr Donnithorne was the director of a nursing home. The building required some renovation and he took charge of the work, paying the workers for invoices that were made out to the nursing home. No profit was made by the appellant who was simply acting as a project manager.

HMRC raised the issue of his position as a contractor and failure to exercise CIS, of which Mr Donnithorne had never heard.

By the time the case reached FTT, HMRC seemed somewhat embarrassed by their position and asked for a decision, which was that all penalties should be quashed.

Case: *Donnithorne v HMRC* [2016] UKFTT 241 (TC)

17. Test cases – how to use the decisions

17.1 Introduction

The outcomes of past cases taken to court and tax tribunals can be used in defending a contractor's position. This can be with HMRC in correspondence when providing responses regarding reasonable excuse – upon receiving notification of the compliance failure – and when requesting an internal review in the event of the officer's decision being against the contractor.

More pertinently, though, these cases need to be reviewed before making the decision to take the case to a First-tier Tax Tribunal, or thereafter to the Upper Tax Tribunal.

One useful quote, though not from a CIS case, is from *Rowland v HMRC*, regarding reasonable excuse:

> "This is a matter to be considered in the light of all the circumstances of the particular case."

Case: *Rowland v HMRC* (2006) SpC 548

17.2 Loss of gross payment status

17.2.1 *Late payment due to cash flow problems*

This assumes a contention by the contractor that the tax payments could not be made on time due to the lack of available funds.

There was a case that HMRC lost in 2005, *Transform Shop Fitters*, where there had been a series of late payments in which, by the lack of action to the contrary, HMRC were held to have acquiesced in the arrangement. Given the stricter rules and the interaction with RTI, this situation is unlikely to recur nowadays.

It is important to establish the facts beforehand, regarding the payments due and the shortage of funds. Bank statements need to be presented as evidence as well as a statement from the bank in respect of the overdraft facility – and, if possible, anything in writing that proves the refusal of any extension.

HMRC will be aware of the cases of *Williams* in 2010 and *Bruce* in 2011, where reference to bank statements proved that funds were available to each of the contractors at the times of the due payments.

Some background in respect of the reason for the shortage of funds is also necessary. In both *Duffy* and *McDowall*, funds had been taken from the business for non-business activities, being property purchases and providing financial assistance to a relative.

HMRC will be looking for evidence of cash flow shortage and why tax was paid late. This is referred to in the guidance as seeking to "counter this natural sympathy" that the Tribunal may have for the contractor. Questions will be asked as to why short-term finance was not sought.

Lack of funds is a common problem in construction, but HMRC will contend that if this is a consistent problem for a contractor, then it is one that (bar the occasional extreme instance) should be managed.

One factor here that has not been tested in tax tribunals is that of employer's National Insurance, which is not a tax on profits but on employment. This applies to all trades but without the issue of loss of GPS with which to contend.

Therefore it is necessary to prove that the payments could not have been made on time. The contractor lost in *Beard* for that lack of evidence. In *Strongwork Construction*, the contractor's injury was a severe incapacity but came after late payments had been made. The contractor lost in *Forsyth* as the bad debt cited also occurred after the late payments.

The contractor lost in *Glen Contract Services* even though the court accepted that collecting payments from clients could be difficult – but the problem here was that insufficient evidence was presented to court to substantiate the claims.

It will be difficult to retain GPS without correct procedure having been followed, and HMRC will be quick to point out the Time to Pay arrangements that exist. This is borne out in *Munns*, thought contrast this with *Kincaid*. The latter may be a useful defence.

No formal arrangements were made for Time to Pay in *Wood*, though the contractor had acted in the same way. GPS was retained, but not necessarily because the FTT thought the actions were reasonable.

However, this can be undermined where arrangements are made with other creditors as, in the 2010 case of *Enderbey Properties*. The contractor lost by not contacting HMRC at the same time, on the same basis.

A strong case can be built on cash flow difficulties to overturn a GPS revocation decision. Though the circumstances were at a time of significant decreases in construction work, the contractor won in *Mutch* by demonstrating how a significant downturn in orders can affect a business, with little opportunity for such a situation to be managed.

Late payments by clients can be a winning card; in *Bannister Combined Services*, payments were held up by local authorities, so the impact on the business by two public sector bodies influenced the court in favour of the contractor.

In *Connaught Contracts*, the business suffered a downturn in contracts but the partners could also show that they had introduced many of their own available funds into the partnership. GPS was retained as they could prove they had done as much as they could.

Joseph-Lester was able to prove that with loss of business, timely tax payments could not be made, and was still able to retain GPS.

There may not need to be one single reason to win on the basis of cash flow shortage; cumulatively, a bad debt, a delayed overdraft and seasonal work fluctuations constituted a reasonable excuse in *PSR Control Systems*. Refer back to the *Rowland* quote at the beginning of the chapter.

Finally, a winning position can be undermined by other factors, such as previous failures and let-offs (*GC Ware Electrics*) or a lack of CIS awareness (*Base Brickwork*).

Cases: *Templeton (HMRC) v Transform Shop Office & Bar Fitters Ltd* [2005] EWHC 1558; *Rowland v HMRC* (2006) SpC 548; *Beard v HMRC* [2009] UKFTT 284 (TC); *Mutch v HMRC* [2009] UKFTT 288 (TC); *Munns v HMRC* [2009] UKFTT 290 (TC); *Strongwork Construction v HMRC* [2009] UKFTT 292 (TC); *Enderbey Properties Ltd v HMRC* [2010] UKFTT 85 (TC); *Bannister Combined Services v HMRC* [2010] UKFTT 158 (TC); *GC Ware Electrics v HMRC* [2010] UKFTT 197 (TC); *Glen Contract Services Ltd v HMRC* [2010] UKFTT 391 (TC); *Williams v HMRC* [2010] UKFTT 508 (TC); *Connaught Contracts (Bennett) v HMRC* [2010] UKFTT 545 (TC); *McDowall v HMRC* [2011] UKFTT 28 (TC); *Joseph-Lester (t/a Scaffold Access Services) v HMRC* [2011] UKFTT 114 (TC); *Wood (t/a Propave) v HMRC* [2011] UKFTT 136 (TC); *Kincaid (t/a AK Construction) v HMRC* [2011] UKFTT 225 (TC); *Bruce (t/a Norrie Bruce Plant Hire) v HMRC* [2011] UKFTT 241 (TC); *Duffy v HMRC* [2011] UKFTT 405 (TC); *Forsyth v HMRC* [2012] UKFTT 209 (TC); *PSR Control Systems Ltd v HMRC* [2012] UKFTT 478 (TC); *Base Brickwork (a firm) v HMRC* [2012] UKFTT 536 (TC)

17.2.2   Reliance on others

The case outcomes in respect of this are not consistent. There may be helpful elements from some of these cases, but in a supporting role. One matter to consider that is evident from the case material, is that a contractor is viewed less sympathetically when an employee or agent is left to undertake the CIS work and it is assumed that this is being done correctly. Some system of review by another staff member or the business owner is not only sensible in itself, but is generally seen as necessary to demonstrate having sufficient regard to CIS compliance.

The contractor won in *Cormac Construction*, where the court was sympathetic to the situation of the wife of a contracting husband, falling behind with payments due to other work and family commitments. This is consistent with HMRC guidance for such businesses. Contrast that though, with *Pollard* where, in similar circumstances, the contractor was not allowed to use his wife's known depression as a reasonable excuse. Similarly in *Steve Jordan Fencing*, the contractor could not fall back on the shortcomings of his mother.

Many contractors employ professionals to look after the affairs of their business. Not all of these, who claim to have knowledge of CIS, know as much as they claim.

The contractor won in *Devon & Cornwall*, with a secretary's absence being held a reasonable excuse for non-compliance – though in conjunction with an acknowledgedly unreliable broadband service.

Another contractor won in *MR Harris Groundworks* where an office manager and an assistant both failed to meet the compliance requirements of the business. They were both replaced and the partners' assurances of increased involvement in the future were accepted.

Reliance on a well-paid consultant was also held to be a reasonable excuse in *RW Westworth*. However, reliance on new accountants was not accepted in *Getty*, nor was it in *Dale Services Contracts*, which produced this quote:

> "... relatively straightforward tasks which are delegated to an agent will not absolve the taxpayer if the agent fails to perform those tasks correctly".

There are no absolutes in this area. It may be argued that with a matter as complex as CIS, the businessman should be able to leave it to staff employed for that function, and to rely on the discretion of HMRC where there are some late payments or submissions.

No doubt HMRC would counter that with the parallel of non-tax business activities, such as a contract being lost or a supply account being terminated, due to delayed actions by members of staff.

Cases: *Cormack (HMRC) v CBL Cable Contractors Ltd* [2005] EWHC 1294; *Devon & Cornwall Surfacing Ltd v HMRC* [2010] UKFTT 199 (TC); *Getty v HMRC* [2010] UKFTT 251 (TC); *Pollard v HMRC* [2010] UKFTT 269 (TC); *MR Harris Groundworks (a partnership) v HMRC* [2010] UKFTT 358 (TC); *RW Westworth Ltd v HMRC* [2010] UKFTT 477 (TC); *Steve Jordan Fencing v HMRC* [2010] UKFTT 570 (TC); *Dale Services Contracts Ltd v HMRC* [2012] UKFTT 299 (TC)

17.2.3   *Proportionality*

In short, do not waste time citing this as a reason. It is for the Tribunal to decide whether the contractor has a reasonable excuse for the compliance failure such that GPS is retained. The Tribunal will say that the rules are set down by Parliament and it is for Parliament to decide whether the effect of GPS revocation is proportionate to the breach of acceptable compliance failures.

The outcome of *Barnes v Hilton Main Construction* has been used many times to rebut claims by contractors that the effect of loss of GPS is out of all proportion to late submission of forms or late payment of tax, where there has been no loss to HM Treasury.

In particular, possession of GPS is not thought to be a human right. It just happens in every industry other than construction.

Case: *Barnes (HMRC) v Hilton Main Construction* [2005] EWHC 1355

17.2.4   *Effect on the business – to 2015*

The guidance regarding GPS was withdrawn from the Revenue booklet IR40 in July 2003, so the powers thereto no longer had to be applied with discretion and common sense, and non-compliance no longer had to be substantial or serious.

This came after *Shaw v Vicky Construction*, where the court agreed with HMRC that the General Commissioners had been too lenient in allowing GPS to be retained by a contractor that scarcely complied with any due dates.

This was compounded by the outcome of *JDC Services* in 2004, where the expectation of future compliance by the GCs was not acceptable and was held to be legally flawed.

The outcome of *Cormack* in 2005 seemed to stem the flow, but this decision was considered to be incorrect in *G-Con* the following year; with the judge siding with the latter in *FAME* a year later.

The slump in construction activity had little effect on decisions, as with *Grosvenor* from which can be quoted:

> "the consequences of cancellation of gross payment status is [sic] not relevant to the issue whether or not there is a reasonable excuse".

But, in 2010, the tide turned with the decision on *Bruns v HMRC*. This is often quoted, regardless of the slightly unusual circumstances of HMRC being unrepresented at the FTT and Mr Bruns being 61 at the time – his being unlikely to obtain employment elsewhere and being a contributor to the taxpayer rather than a burden, and also that the sale of his machinery would bring about a severe loss. From this hearing:

> "An excuse can arguably be regarded as reasonable by reference to the consequences of the withdrawal of gross payment status. This would be the case where such a withdrawal would, on the facts, be a disproportionate sanction for the non-compliance in question."

There were other factors to consider in *Bruns*, particularly cash flow pressures and family issues. However the judge chose to make a stand on behalf of contractors, going on to say that the consequences of GPS loss would be disproportionate to the late payment of tax (compensated by interest charges), and that "this factor could well render the Appellant's excuse reasonable even if ... there was no other basis on which his excuse could be held to be reasonable."

This needs to be made subtly distinct from a simple claim of disproportionality. The FTT accepted that Mr Bruns' business would cease as his two main clients did not wish to trade with a non-compliant subbie. This is not the same as losing some business.

However, this did open the door slightly, and it opened a little further with the outcome of *S Morris Groundwork* in 2010. A company with a turnover of £4.5m stood to lose a contract worth £3.2m if GPS were to be withdrawn, jeopardising the future of 100 employees. The judge sided with *Bruns* and GPS was retained.

These findings did not help the contractor in *Shaw Cleaning v HMRC* 2011 – neither case was quoted, though HMRC did cite *Grosvenor*, and GPS was lost.

Cases: *Shaw (HMRC) v Vicky Construction Ltd* [2002] EWHC 2659; *Hudson (HMRC) v JDC Services Ltd* [2004] EWHC 602; *Cormack (HMRC) v CBL Cable Contractors Ltd* [2005] EWHC 1294; *Arnold (HMRC) v G-Con Ltd* [2005] & [2006] EWCA Civ 829; *HMRC v Facilities and Maintenance Engineering Ltd (FAME)* [2006] EWHC 689; *Grosvenor v HMRC* [2009] UKFTT 283 (TC); *Bruns (t/a TK Fabrications) v HMRC* [2010] UKFTT 58 (TC); *S Morris Groundwork Ltd v HMRC* [2010] UKFTT 585 (TC); *Scofield v HMRC* [2011] UKFTT 199 (TC); *Shaw Cleaning Services v HMRC* [2011] UKFTT 378 (TC); *JP Whitter (Waterwell Engineers) Ltd v HMRC* [2012] UKFTT 278 (TC); *John Kerr Roofing Contractors v HMRC* [2013] UKFTT 135 (TC)

17.2.5 Effect on the business – 2015 onwards

Following *S Morris Groundwork*, the prospects for contractors improved yet further with *JP Whitter*. The contractor did not have a good record of compliance and had been allowed to retain GPS before; HMRC won at FTT in April 2012, but the contractor appealed and the case was reheard in August 2012.

The contractor as before claimed that loss of GPS could mean the end of the business with 50-75% of contracts being lost. Where HMRC lost was by acknowledging that this could happen, but contended that this could not be taken into account with the decision (to revoke GPS). The Tribunal considered this to be a relevant factor and as such the earlier decision was wrong in law. The contractor retained GPS.

After years of denying the effect of GPS revocation, HMRC were faced with the prospect of having to accept that the future of the business was a relevant factor. Rather than being treated as a maverick case, as with *Cormack*, the *Whitter* decision was cited and upheld a few months later in *John Kerr Roofing*. As with *Whitter*, this case also took into account the issues of discretion covered in *Scofield*.

This made the issue of loss of GPS more widely known. Several public sector bodies have stated openly that they will only accept tenders from businesses with GPS. It would be quite possible for a contractor in a subcontracting role to obtain something in correspondence from their client, stating the importance of GPS and using this as a shield against its loss.

This situation was unacceptable to HMRC, which therefore took *Whitter* to the Upper Tax Tribunal.

HMRC disputed the FTT's view that the decision to revoke, ignoring relevant factors such as the effect on the business, was wrong in law – which would allow FTT to substitute their own view. Their contention was that there was no requirement to consider the effect on the business.

Whitter's barrister invoked human rights legislation insofar as under s. 66, HMRC would need to exercise discretion in order to be compliant with this, and in order for the effect of revocation to be proportionate.

In the end, the UTT judges sided with HMRC in that there was no express direction made in CIS regarding financial effect of revocation, and given the doubt that that brought into the FTT decision, allowed HMRC's appeal.

The company directors weighed up the consequences and took their case to the Court of Appeal. This, at least, allowed them to retain GPS in the meantime.

Both sides retained the same barrister – being from the same Chambers, the company's Counsel being the junior of HMRC's. The company's main argument was that UTT erred in their decision, in that HMRC were required to exercise discretion proportionately.

Some of the consideration by UTT in terms of s. 66 and human rights was questioned, but the principal blow to the company's case was the view from the leading Court of Appeal judge that:

> "I cannot find any indication … that Parliament intended HMRC to have the power, and still less a duty, to take into account matters extraneous to the CIS regime."

Were this the case, it would have been expressly stated and with some guidance. Furthermore, "[the company] will have nobody to blame but itself if its registration for gross payment is cancelled".

The company's appeal was dismissed and, one would assume, it lost GPS for a twelve-month period.

Two observations to be made are as follows. Firstly, it does not seem as though the company's Counsel made any mention of HMRC's original policy (to be found in **Appendix 2** of this book), nor its quiet elimination from their guidance to contractors. Might the pursuance of questioning HMRC's policy have made a difference to the outcome?

Secondly, in the interests of balance, it should be said that at the time of writing the company is still trading. As far as can be gleaned from abbreviated accounts submitted to Companies House, there has been no rapid decrease of retained profits – but this gives no idea of how turnover and the workforce may have been affected.

Cases: *Cormack (HMRC) v CBL Cable Contractors Ltd* [2005] EWHC 1294; *S Morris Groundwork Ltd v HMRC* [2010] UKFTT 585 (TC); *Scofield v HMRC* [2011] UKFTT 199 (TC); *JP Whitter (Waterwell Engineers) Ltd v HMRC* [2012] UKFTT 278 (TC); *John Kerr Roofing Contractors v HMRC* [2013] UKFTT 135 (TC); *HMRC v JP Whitter (Waterwell Engineers) Ltd* [2015] UKUT 392 (TCC); *JP Whitter (Waterwell Engineers) Ltd v HMRC* [2016] EWCA Civ 1160

17.2.6   Technicalities

Appealing GPS revocation on this basis is risky. It is also likely to involve a lot of legal costs. However, there has been some success for contractors.

In *Scofield*, it was argued that HMRC's automated process whereby a letter was sent to the contractor setting out the compliance failures and advising loss of GPS, did not constitute any application of discretion by HMRC. The contractor would have lost GPS on the facts presented, so this may well have been value for money – HMRC lost their appeal in 2011 – but by discovering an inconsistency between the law and actual procedures, *Scofield* helped many other contractors and effected a change in the HMRC system. Letters are now sent allowing 30 days to offer a reasonable excuse, to which discretion is to be applied.

The contractor also won in *Ithell*. It was claimed that no notice of GPS revocation had been received by the contractor or his accountant. The decision turned on the inability of HMRC to produce a copy of the notice to the FTT. It is questionable whether such an omission could be relied upon.

Cases: *Ithell v HMRC* [2011] UKFTT 155 (TC); *Scofield v HMRC* [2011] UKFTT 199 (TC)

17.3   Penalties

17.3.1   Introduction

Given the costs of preparing for and attending a First-tier Tax Tribunal, it should be considered whether the likely effect on any penalties levied would be worthwhile. It could be a costly principle to have upheld. Bear in mind that penalties are decided on the basis of the late submission; it is that same record that will be reviewed for GPS renewal, so it may only be worthwhile seeking to have penalties overturned for a reasonable excuse should GPS need to be applied for or sought within the next twelve months.

17.3.2 Complexity and burden of CIS

When considering an appeal, it is worth comparing the circumstances of the case with those in *Barking Brickwork*. The findings of the FTT could be most helpful, especially in the case of a smaller contractor – in particular, the observations concerning guidance and the volume of information in respect of CIS.

But the responsibility of managing CIS has to be taken seriously; a careful choice of words is also important, so claims of being too busy can be costly.

Cases: *Barking Brickwork Contractors Ltd v HMRC* [2015] UKFTT 260 (TC); *Alpine Contract Service Ltd v HMRC* [2016] UKFTT 394 (TC)

17.3.3 Proportionality

As a defence in itself, claiming that the penalties are disproportionate to the offence will not work. It would not be a sound idea to assume that the FTT will take pity. Refer to the 2011 case of *KD Ductworks*, in which the findings in *Stubbs* were cited regarding the application of law, fairness and equality.

The most notable case was that of *Bosher v HMRC* in 2012, where the FTT decided to undertake its own application of fairness and recalculated penalties with regard to the non-compliance; HMRC later appealed successfully for their own (already mitigated) figure to apply.

Sometimes, though, this can work. In *Laithwaite*, the FTT weighed up the penalties in comparison to the contractor's profits and chose to find that there was a reasonable excuse for the late submissions.

HMRC will contend that though they have power of mitigation in respect of CIS penalties, the FTT has no such jurisdiction; but this point was not agreed by the judges in *Turner* in 2014.

The FTT found that they did have jurisdiction, on those penalties levied in respect of returns more than twelve months late, in the 2010 case of *Lewis*.

In *Thomas Dalziel*, the circumstances of the husband and wife running the business were taken into account, in that the FTT found that reasonable excuse should result in a halving of the penalties.

Given the recent moves by HMRC not to charge penalties for nil returns, an appeal may be considered worthwhile if a back-dating cannot be applied. The contractor was partially successful in *Westwood Houses*, where the FTT reduced the penalty in that it had been raised for nil returns.

Finally, an application to HMRC for penalties to be mitigated prior to any FTT, citing some of the test cases as applicable to circumstances, may prove beneficial.

Cases: *Stubbs v HMRC* (2007) SpC 638; *Lewis v HMRC* [2010] UKFTT 327 (TC); *KD Ductworks Installations v HMRC* [2011] UKFTT 76 (TC); *Westwood Houses Ltd v HMRC* [2012] UKFTT 166 (TC); *Bosher v HMRC* [2012] UKFTT 631 (TC); *Thomas Dalziel Steelfixing & Formwork v HMRC* [2014] UKFTT 725 (TC); *Laithwaite v HMRC* [2014] UKFTT 759 (TC); *Turner v HMRC* [2014] UKFTT 1124 (TC)

17.3.4   *Reliance on others*

Included under this heading is the Post Office; not that this applies now with the abolition of paper returns, but some contractors still make payments by cheque. Generally, a lack of proof of postage will weaken any application for penalties to be set aside.

In *First In Service*, HMRC's system of dealing with incoming post was discussed and accepted as satisfactory, as was the case in *PG Glazing*. This followed the case of *Heronslea* where HMRC were unable to provide the FTT with a date-stamped copy of the return, therefore the penalty was cancelled; this defence proved effective in other cases. This was taken further in *Oddy* in 2014, with a successful outcome for the contractor.

As with the GPS cases above, it is risky to assume that HMRC will not have necessary evidence available.

It was held in *MEM Industrial Roofing* that HMRC cannot impose proof of postage as a requirement for penalty cancellation, though their case was undermined by a lack of evidence presented to the FTT.

Reliance on staff or accountants can be successful; penalties were reduced in part in the cases of *Bells Mills Developments, Contour Business Interiors, MCM2 Cladding* and *Sowinski*. In *Laithwaite*, penalties were mitigated by HMRC on account of the incorrect advice provided by the accountant, before the FTT eliminated them entirely, as was the case in *Barrett* – this last case proving the benefit of the appellant having well-informed advisers.

However, reliance without supervision did not prove to be a reasonable excuse in *Austin* in 2010, nor for *Savage* in 2014, *B&I Plastering* in 2015 or *Thompson Heating* in 2016; the admission of blame by the accountant in *Iles* did not work either. Being too busy to provide information to the accountant was costly in *ASM*.

Reliance on an agency, which failed to communicate in respect of the payment of deductions, was only partially successful in *CJS Eastern*, but more successful in *Barking Brickwork*.

Cases: *Bells Mills Developments Ltd v HMRC* [2009] UKFTT 390 (TC); *Austin v HMRC* [2010] UKFTT 312 (TC); *Heronslea Ltd v HMRC* [2011] UKFTT 102 (TC); *Contour Business Interiors v HMRC* [2011] UKFTT 300 (TC); *PG Glazing Ltd v HMRC* [2011] UKFTT 562 (TC); *MEM Industrial Roofing Ltd v HMRC* [2011] UKFTT 604 (TC); *First in Service Ltd v HMRC* [2012] UKFTT 250 (TC); *Iles (t/a Purbeck Plumbing Heating & Drainage) v HMRC* [2012] UKFTT 389 (TC); *Savage (Savage Electrics Ltd) v HMRC* [2014] UKFTT 521 (TC); *Oddy (t/a CMO Bird Proofing Specialists) v HMRC* [2014] UKFTT 673 (TC); *Laithwaite v HMRC* [2014] UKFTT 759 (TC); *CJS Eastern Ltd v HMRC* [2015] UKFTT 213 (TC); *Barking Brickwork Contractors Ltd v HMRC* [2015] UKFTT 260 (TC); *MCM2 Cladding Systems Ltd v HMRC* [2015] UKFTT 254 (TC); *Barrett v HMRC* [2015] UKFTT 329 (TC); *B&I Plastering v HMRC* [2015] UKFTT 587 (TC); *Sowinski v HMRC* [2015] UKFTT 636 (TC); *Thompson Heating (2000) Ltd v HMRC* [2016] UKFTT 165 (TC); *ASM (Refurbishments & Decorators) Ltd v HMRC* [2016] UKFTT 822 (TC)

17.3.5 Technicalities

The contractor argued successfully that photocopies of CIS returns were acceptable as being in the same format as those issued by HMRC, and penalties were cancelled in *Scotts Glass*.

Penalties were reduced in *Project Developments*, where HMRC took some time in issuing duplicate returns.

Initially in *Westwood Houses*, the contractor argued that for nil returns, no penalty should apply in that £100 per 50 contractors should be the same as £100 times nil. This element of the defence was not accepted.

It can be worth verifying HMRC's evidence for raising penalties, as long as the contractor has his own evidence of submission to identify discrepancies. The FTT cited the importance of the integrity of HMRC's own records in *PM Reinforcements*.

Cases: *Scotts Glass & Glazing Services v HMRC* [2011] UKFTT 508 (TC); *Westwood Houses Ltd v HMRC* [2012] UKFTT 166 (TC); *Project Developments (South Wales) Ltd v HMRC* [2012] UKFTT 322 (TC); *PM Reinforcements Ltd v HMRC* [2017] UKFTT 434 (TC)

17.3.6   Other factors

There may be something very unusual that can be construed as a reasonable excuse. The contractor in *Stone* had all penalties dismissed, as he was running a business despite receiving dialysis treatment. However, contrast this with *North* where, as with *Pollard* in the GPS case above, the ongoing illness of the wife (and bookkeeper) of the contractor was not regarded as a reasonable excuse or as special circumstances.

There was a partial reduction in penalties in *Koleychuk* due to the contractor's limited grasp of English and reliance on an interpreter. Implicit in this, though, is an assumption that full CIS compliance is to be achieved at some point.

The scope of CIS came into play in *Parkinson*, where a gardener/landscaper was unaware that the scheme applied to his workers – penalties were reduced by the FTT.

One circumstance on its own may not be enough, but several together may win the day, as with *Scott*, but not always as in *Dobbs*.

For issues such as materials and reg. 9, the pertinent cases are quoted in the specific chapters.

Cases: *Pollard v HMRC* [2010] UKFTT 269 (TC); *Stone v HMRC* [2010] UKFTT 414 (TC); *Koleychuk v HMRC* [2012] UKFTT 224 (TC); *North v HMRC* [2015] UKFTT 56 (TC); *Parkinson v HMRC* [2015] UKFTT 342 (TC); *Scott Building Contracts Ltd v HMRC* [2017] UKFTT 630 (TC); *Dobbs v HMRC* [2017] UKFTT 163 (TC)

17.4   Other taxes

Any business that has suffered an excess of CIS deductions may have that excess sum repaid, or offset against other liabilities. As mentioned in **12.10** above, a formal claim must be made to HMRC for an offset.

Without such a claim, appeals against late payment penalties or surcharges are likely to fail. It may be possible to mitigate these if it can be proven that HMRC have not acted in accordance with their own procedures or guidelines.

Cases: *Graffiti Busters Ltd v HMRC* [2014] UKFTT 61 (TC); *French Polish Ltd v HMRC* [2014] UKFTT 91 (TC); *MPH Joinery Ltd v HMRC* [2015] UKFTT 106 (TC); *UPR Services Ltd v HMRC* [2015] UKFTT 415 (TC); *Quality Asbestos Services Ltd* [2015] UKFTT 595 (TC); *GH Preston Partnership v HMRC* [2016] UKFTT 296 (TC); *SOS Joinery Ltd v HMRC* [2016] UKFTT 535 (TC); *Paul Raymond Marsh v HMRC* [2007] UKVAT V20091

18. Improving the operation of the Construction Industry Scheme – the 2014 consultation

18.1 Introduction

Following discussions at ministerial level regarding CIS in late 2013, HMRC issued a consultation document in June 2014. The foreword mentions the commitment to make the tax system easier, quicker and simpler for businesses.

There was no mention in the foreword about making CIS easier for HMRC, who were allowed to set the agenda and did so within a very narrow frame. Though the principal headings covered GPS, monthly returns, verification and the new idea of an online account for deductions, the areas covered were of more interest to HMRC.

18.2 Outcomes

The outcomes of the consultation were as follows:

April 2015	no penalties for nil returns; GPS for all parties to joint ventures; online appeals for penalties.
April 2016	reduction in GPS threshold to £100,000 for multiple partner/director businesses; mandatory online filing of monthly returns; directors' SA payments, Class 1A NIC and corporation tax payments no longer included in GPS compliance tests.
April 2017	mandatory online verification.

No date was given for the digitally integrated online account, and in March 2017 HMRC said that, despite previous assurances that the work was on schedule, this facility would not be provided at any time in the near future. This would have been of great benefit for those subcontractors who have not received deduction statements or who may have mislaid them. The date of submission of deduction could then be checked against the date of payment, with any delays reported to HMRC, especially where that disadvantages the subcontractor for the deduction falling into a later year or later than a requested set-off against other liabilities.

This would also have assisted subcontractors in obtaining repayments of surplus CIS deductions, such that records held by HMRC can be reviewed in-year and queried as necessary, rather than waiting for problems to emerge after 5 April.

18.3 Details of the outcomes

18.3.1 Returns

This forced over 30,000 contractors, accustomed to paper returns, to make online submissions from April 2016, as with RTI, VAT and corporation tax. HMRC exercised an element of leniency in the early months, but now the penalty regime applies fully.

18.3.2 Verifications

This is an issue for both contractors and subcontractors. It is clear from past statistics that the online service has not been as accurate as it should be; there were 10% of unmatched online verifications logged, but only 1-2% of deductions were made at the higher rate.

This seems to derive from differences in spellings, which HMRC refer to as "fuzzy name matching". Such differences can be overcome when speaking to a person, and clearly have been. HMRC are apparently aiming to improve the name recognition element of the online service.

The telephone service will be largely withdrawn from April 2017, though a reduced service will remain available. Therefore it is in their best interests that contractors report problems to HMRC with regard to online matching problems, in order that the online service is improved from its past performance.

18.3.3 Gross payment status

The tests from April 2016 focus on compliance regarding CIS returns, CIS and PAYE/employer deductions, and IT/CT returns. The reference to employer deductions includes both National Insurance and student loan obligations.

This still represents many areas for which errors could jeopardise GPS. There is also the matter of failure to issue deduction statements that has already lost some contractors their GPS, though

HMRC seem to bracket this within the heading of "non-compliance of such severity" that can lead to revocation of GPS at any time.

These changes can hardly be regarded as "substantially fewer obligations" as claimed in the consultation's summary of responses. Contractors still need to be aware of those obligations and to have sound procedures in place, to protect the future of the business but also the employees on whom a significant responsibility is placed.

The reduction in the turnover threshold for multi-principal contractors is a very small shift in enabling such businesses to register for GPS, affecting between 400 and 1,000 businesses. There are over 50,000 contractors operating without GPS; HMRC declined the initiative to contact those businesses directly to encourage application.

Arguably the retention of the £30,000 minimum – for services excluding materials – at the 2007 level, has allowed more businesses to register, though given the downturn in the industry and the competition in prices and margin, there may not have been much inflationary erosion of this barrier.

18.3.4   Penalties

HMRC have offered some flexibility in this area, in backdating rules when the new system of penalties was introduced in 2012, and have also allowed backdating of nil return periods claimed late, after some missed nil returns.

The new initiative allows for the cancellation of a penalty for a nil return. However, it has first to be established that the return for the period in question was a nil return. It is less hassle to appeal – online – for cancellation of a penalty than going to FTT to make the claim. The obligation of making that return remains.

It also gives rise to the scenario of a less than scrupulous contractor declaring many deductions in one month and suffering one penalty – which could greatly affect the subcontractors concerned.

18.4   Impact of the consultation

The most disappointing element of this process is that a consultation is now recorded as having taken place. The principal changes to CIS are those that benefit HMRC – notably mandatory online filing of monthly returns (so no further need to issue pre-populated paper returns) and the downgrading of the telephone verification service.

These steps could have been taken without the consultation and have been forced through regardless of preferences to the contrary. It is difficult to be anything but cynical when observing that these steps have been spun as being the outcome of a consultation with all interested parties.

What has been offered in return are really crumbs off the king's table. The loosening of regulation will have very little impact on the contractors and subcontractors operating within CIS.

The consultation has not fulfilled the main purpose, which was to "substantially reduce CIS businesses' administrative costs". Indeed, the net effect will have been an increase, given the time that 30,000 contractors have needed to spend to learn about online submissions, as well as the time that contractors spend waiting on the much-reduced telephone service to make or check a verification.

HMRC have failed the industry in not providing the digital account for subcontractors – this was first mentioned publicly in June 2014 (and referred to long prior to that). Until it is in place – which the equivalent Irish system has had since 2012 – the consultation can only be seen as a sham.

Case: *Scotts Glass & Glazing Services v HMRC* [2011] UKFTT 508 (TC)

19. CIS equivalents in other countries

19.1 Introduction

Many other countries have taxes in respect of ownership of real estate or rents. This chapter will only look at those tax laws that relate to construction operations.

It is not just in the UK that a scheme particular to the construction industry operates. This will not necessarily be an exhaustive list – as some worldwide tax guides make no specific mention of CIS in covering the UK tax system, it can be difficult to ascertain the workings of other countries. Therefore these are included for interest as opposed to guidance in undertaking construction operations overseas.

19.2 Republic of Ireland

The Irish system has been in place for many years and has many similarities to the UK CIS. There are definitions of contractor and subcontractor, rules for gross payment status and the deduction of tax at source at the standard rate (20%) and the higher rate (35%). This higher rate applies to unregistered subcontractors, or those with an inadequate tax compliance record. It also applies to non-resident subcontractors unless Irish tax registration is obtained, though a refund may be applied for from the Revenue.

The equivalent of GPS is to be a zero rate subcontractor. This requires full tax compliance for a three year period.

Tax deducted is known as Relevant Contract Tax (RCT) which is paid monthly within strict time frames to the Irish Revenue. This tax is redeemed by the subcontractor primarily against income or corporation tax. It can also be offset against PAYE and VAT. There are penalties due if the contractor does not make the monthly or quarterly return on time. The contractor must pay the higher rate of tax should the correct rate of tax not be applied to the payment.

There are some differences, and it is interesting to see how the Irish Revenue have designed their system.

Each contract is registered by the contractor separately, even if there are several with the same subcontractor. Payments can only be made online for registered contracts. Part of the registration process includes a detailed questionnaire regarding the circumstances of the engagement of the subcontractor. Every payment made to a subcontractor needs to be reported to the Revenue.

There are closer links to VAT than in the UK, and the system applies to businesses in the construction industry as well as those engaged in forestry and meat processing operations.

The Irish system became entirely online in 2012, but with a difference that makes it more advanced than the UK CIS.

When submissions are made using the Revenue Online System (ROS), a copy of the deduction authorisation is generated by the Revenue and the contractor needs to give a copy to the subcontractor. However, the subcontractor can also register with the ROS, which gives sight of all transactions logged in his name, including the rate of deduction. A rate review can be requested if thought necessary.

The Irish Revenue have combined online mandatory filing with the online access that HMRC are considering, but have not promised, when monthly returns become mandatory in April 2016.

19.3   Australia

The Australian system operates more closely to their equivalent of the UK PAYE system, known as Pay As You Go (PAYG). Employees are recognised as such, but there is also a category for labour-hire workers. A test applies to subcontractors to determine whether a worker needs to be classed as labour only and indeed genuinely self-employed. There are different rates that apply depending on the regularity of payment as well as allowances and expenses.

For subcontracting construction businesses that are recognised as such, there are no deductions of tax at source.

The Australian Tax Office realised that their system was burdensome for businesses, therefore contractors now only need to make annual returns of gross payments to subcontractors, this being a change from the previous quarterly system.

Their online system has versions of the UK ESI tool, with one specifically designed for those in building and construction, to distinguish between employees and contractors.

One notable difference with the Australian system is that contractors – that is, the self-employed – can enter into a voluntary arrangement with the payer such that tax is deducted at source, as a saving scheme for their own tax liabilities. This is a flexible arrangement, left to the two parties to agree between themselves and that may be terminated at any time by either side.

19.4 Germany

The Federal Central Tax Office administers a system of withholding tax on construction activities. This was introduced in 2002 and appears to have been closely modelled on the UK CIS. It has many features in common; there is a rate of withholding tax (15%) which the contractor must collect, or if not is liable for the sum due, though subcontractors may obtain an exemption certificate. Construction activities are defined much as in the UK, with non-construction activities included if part of an overall project.

In practice, an exemption certificate is not too difficult to obtain, there being no minimum turnover levels. This scheme was brought in to curb tax lost from unregistered workers from within Germany but more importantly from other countries. Readers familiar with the TV series *Auf Wiedersehen Pet* would recognise this situation. HMRC certainly did – the actor Tim Healy from that series was used in radio advertising in the lead-up to the CIS launch of 2007. This was before HMRC took him to the FTT to deny tax relief on accommodation costs.

19.5 Gibraltar

Again similar to the UK system, where a scheme exists that recognises construction subcontractors from which 25% of labour costs must be deducted, subject to presentation of an exemption certificate granted on the record of tax compliance and the existence of a business. Tax certificates must be provided as proof of the deduction.

19.6   Canada

The Canada Revenue Agency has in place a Contract Payment Reporting System. Any business that has construction as its main business activity must report each year, total payments made to each subcontractor with their tax references. This can be by calendar or fiscal year and needs to be submitted within six months of the period end. No tax is deducted from self-employed subcontractors.

19.7   Other countries

The US Internal Revenue Service appear to be more concerned with accounting rules around the tax year end regarding ongoing contracts and the timing of payments for construction projects. No deductions of tax are made from construction subcontractors.

Countries that operate a withholding tax from payments specifically for construction operations, from both residents and non-residents, are:

Angola	3.5%
Ecuador	1% (also applicable to other trades)
Gambia	10% (where a contractor pays a subcontractor)
Indonesia	2-6%
Malawi	4%
Nigeria	5%
Pakistan	6%
Seychelles	5%
Sri Lanka	0.25-1% (Guarantee Fund levy)

In Belgium, a main contractor needs to establish that a subcontractor has no unpaid Belgian tax debts. If there are such debts, those amounts (up to 50% of the payment due to the subbie) must be deducted and paid over to the Federal Public Service. Otherwise, the contractor or potentially the end client may be liable for those unpaid taxes.

Zimbabwe has a basic deduction of 10% for all taxpayers that do not hold a tax clearance certificate, granted when all returns and payments are up to date. Such a method was mentioned in the OTS self-employment report, though without any figures in terms of the cost to business.

20. The future of the Construction Industry Scheme

20.1 Introduction

There will come a time when CIS is abolished. Not long after that time, most people will look back with surprise that such a scheme was imposed on one industry, for so long and at such cost.

20.2 Past and present

The 1975-1999 scheme was less burdensome and with a greater breadth of discretion built into the HMRC guidance. The General Commissioners were there to correct any over-zealous decisions. There was no survey similar to that undertaken by KPMG in 2006 to assess the cost of that version of CIS, but it seems fair to assume it would have been the least costly of the three.

The move to self-assessment in 1997 brought in a snappier culture for the Revenue; tax collected more quickly, the rise in the number and perceived importance of forms, penalties applied even when no tax was lost from late compliance. CIS followed that tide with the second and ill-fated 1999-2007 version of the scheme; the possibility of its abolition was lost in the need for its revision. The increase in bureaucracy in all walks of life assured its continuance into the scheme we have now.

CIS is not a tax. It is a method of ensuring that tax is collected, with the identification of earnings as a by-product, though one that HMRC does not often exploit.

The costs of CIS to the construction industry, as well as the resources used by HMRC in its administration – recently estimated (by HMRC) to be an incredibly low figure of £15 million per year – need to be balanced against the risk of tax being lost from the non-declaration of earnings.

There are some people involved in construction that operate off the grid or below the radar, but far fewer than 40 years ago. There is a lot more recognition of health and safety issues. Insurance is taken more seriously, which tends to lead to a lot of overlap of cover. Possession of a CSCS card is almost mandatory to gain access to a recognised construction site.

Deaths on UK construction sites have decreased to around 50 per year from the stringent enforcement of increasingly prescriptive safety rules. Within the scope of the "industry", as opposed to work in the domestic sector, there are far fewer cowboy operators these days.

Sometimes the construction industry does not help itself. There has been cartel behaviour with some of the larger firms; the frameworks arguably protect those larger firms by keeping the smaller, ambitious firms in their place. Some employees have been blacklisted for acting on behalf of unions. Land has been retained and revalued upwards each year rather than used to build houses.

After 2008, construction was one sector that the banks were reluctant to finance, overdrafts becoming a rare commodity. With the lack of backing and little profit margin, the industry turned on itself with subcontractors having longer credit terms imposed on reduced payments, with many going bust. Suppliers reduced their credit terms either to survive or as dictated by their credit insurers.

But none of this impacts on the payment of subcontractors. It has been established from the Ipsos MORI survey of 2010 that there are far fewer payments made by cash. Security vans with blokes in helmets turning up with the Friday wage money belong to episodes of *The Sweeney* rather than the modern method of direct transfers to bank accounts.

So surely it is those remaining cash payments where the risk lies. For such a small percentage to gear an industry into bearing a quarter of a billion pounds of admin each year seems unreasonable and unnecessary. If payments are made to businesses in receipt of invoices or applications for payment into traceable bank accounts, why should those payments be treated any differently to any other business simply because of the nature of the work?

20.3 Justification of CIS

The risk of tax loss arising from the payment of large numbers of self-employed subcontractors needs to be weighed up dispassionately. This is not something that can be left to HMRC or HM Treasury. The estimates of the cost to industry were so far off – £52m compared to £321m, according to KPMG in 2006 – and in the direction that favours the retention of CIS, that an independent assessment would be needed.

The issue of the number of workers in self-employment – still about 800,000 – is used to justify the continuation of CIS. Clearly, this is an entirely different issue. The Office of Tax Simplification (OTS), in March 2015, issued a weighty Employment Status Report on the whole issue of self-employment, but stepped back from commenting on CIS, referring to the 2014 consultation as well as the scheme being outside the remit of the Report. If that separation can be made, then CIS can be assessed purely in terms of security of tax collection.

That number of 800,000 was established by the OTS in 2014, before the impact had been assessed of the Onshore Intermediaries legislation with came into force in April 2014. Many agencies at that time moved workers away from self-employment payment methods, on to umbrella employment schemes.

Yield statistics from CIS can make interesting reading. Up to 2013-14, annual yield was about £4 billion, being £2.4 billion from individuals and £1.6 billion from other trading entities. Self-employment across all industries has increased, and yield from CIS now exceeds £5 billion. There was a change of rules in expenses for umbrella workers beginning in April 2015. This may explain a shift back to self-employment, an area which is receiving more attention under the heading of the "gig economy".

The demand for housebuilding has driven an upward trend in construction activity, though statistics issued seem remarkably inconsistent, often with a failure to take account of seasonal factors.

CIS remains in place, and despite one or two hints, it has yet to be duplicated for any other industry.

20.4   The half billion pound rip-off

The annual cost to the industry of administering CIS used to be higher, as revealed in the 2006 KPMG report, but is now around £250m as calculated in **Appendix 1**. There is no other industry-specific scheme that comes even close to this level of cost.

Penalty farming is an accusation regularly levelled at HMRC, and though those levied through CIS have been tempered and capped, this can still mean thousands payable by businesses for late compliance.

There is also the cost to the industry of the denial of reg. 9, where tax is paid on occasion by both contractor and subcontractor.

However, the worst cost to the industry is the tax deducted and paid to HMRC, but not redeemed. This was known about but carefully concealed, until a Freedom of Information request in October 2013 revealed that in the three years to 2009-10, the "balance of CIS deductions awaiting allocation" were £371m, £392m and £268m respectively – a total of just over £1bn.

Since then, HMRC have admitted that the current equivalent annual sum is between £300m and £400m. In February 2014, an analysis of how these figures arise was promised. Since then, no figures or explanations have been provided.

It would appear that much as HMRC consider that half an hour per week of a minimum wage earner is enough for a contractor to administer CIS, then the same resource is sufficient to look into this matter. One might imagine that if HMRC were underpaid by the same amount, more effort would be put into its investigation. A request by a member of the House of Commons Public Accounts Committee into the analysis and how HMRC may approach the reconciliation and repayment of these sums never received a reply of any substance.

If, as mentioned in **Chapter 15**, a proportion of the unredeemed total is attributed to companies that are not interested in compliance and accept the deductions, and subcontractors that have returned to their country of origin satisfied with whatever net pay has been received, that is still likely to leave a considerable amount of unredeemed tax withheld from those who feel it should not be claimed for lack of a deduction statement, or who are unaware of the repayment that may be due. For HMRC, this is easy money and helps to bump up the overall tax yield.

Aggregating the cost of CIS, penalties and tax levied and – for want of any useful information from HMRC to the contrary – a significant proportion of the unredeemed tax, it seems fair to say that CIS costs the construction industry half a billion pounds each year. This is about the same as retailers suffer from shoplifters.

It really is high time that this was recognised for the unfair rip-off it is.

20.5   Alternatives to CIS

If there is a desire to reduce the administrative burden on business, then HM Government could do worse than to abolish CIS. In addition, as with scrap metal payments, there should be a ban on cash payments for non-administrative services.

That leaves the risk of subcontractors being paid, but choosing not to declare all income received. What might provide some assurance against that?

The systems run by the Australian Tax Office and the Canada Revenue Service may have the answer. Each year, contractors must make a declaration of payments made to subcontractors. If such a list identified the subcontractor by UTR and the bank accounts to where payments were made, this can be compared to the subcontractors' own declarations of earnings. This would still provide a greater level of declaration than that which exists for the other 3.3 million self-employed people not in construction (according to the OTS report).

Failure to obtain or declare correctly those details, could expose the contractor to making the equivalent tax payment as under reg. 13 at present. This would focus the penalty of non-compliance on those miscreant businesses rather than burdening the whole of the industry with an expensive scheme with which the majority comply in full anyway.

HMRC here is cast in the role of an inefficient teacher that keeps the whole class in after school, rather than dealing with the two hooligans at the back. The rest of the class is doing nothing wrong, but there are penalties only if they do.

The Australian system does include the provision for tax deduction for labour-only workers. This is unnecessary and inappropriate – not least with the verdict in *Hall v Lorimer*, where the worker is engaged for his skills, but also because it is impractical to try to make alternative definitions. This is why the 2009 consultation *False self-employment in construction* came to nothing – because of a lack of understanding of the workings of the industry.

The Onshore Intermediaries legislation is aimed at closing down the less reputable agencies; therefore there already is a tool by which an individual under supervision, direction and control must be an employee. Whatever the outcome of the OTS Report, the construction industry must retain the ability to engage and disengage labour and services on a flexible basis.

As can be seen from **Chapter 19**, the majority of developed countries do not feel a need for special rules for their construction industry. The most prescriptive and highest taxed country is Ireland; at the risk of treading on thin ice, perhaps that country has its own issues with which to deal, and some itinerant workers may have contributed to the problems identified in the early 1970s.

20.6   Responsibilities of HMRC

Rather than pass on responsibility to the industry at enormous cost, HMRC must do their job. The resources devoted to managing CIS can be more gainfully directed to the black economy, and in particular domestic construction where cash payments abound.

In all other trades, there will be businesses that make late submissions and pay their taxes late. It is assumed that the current structure of penalties and interest is a sufficient deterrent, especially now that penalties under RTI are in force. Why should that not apply to construction, equally and no more? It has been proven in court that the threat of loss of GPS can jeopardise the future of a business. The impact is out of all proportion to the offence, particularly when no tax has been lost. Yet the recent consultation on CIS considered this to be vital, to protect the tax yield.

Construction has been treated badly by HMRC. The billions of unredeemed deductions in recent years remain unexplained. Nothing was done for years to help subcontractors prove their deductions. The digital online account for subcontractors (as a substitute for deduction statements) has still not been introduced, three years after the idea was proposed in the 2014 consultation, and there is no firm timeframe for its implementation.

However, the Irish Revenue have had such a system in place since 2012, introduced at the same time as mandatory online filing. This has been achieved despite massive cuts in public sector spending in that country.

HMRC had their chance with the 2014 consultation and have done what suited them under the guise and spin of helping construction businesses. If HMG is serious about reducing administrative burdens, then a new consultation is needed to review alternatives to CIS, to have an unbiased discussion of whether a construction-specific scheme is required, and to give the industry the opportunity to make its opinion known.

21. SI 2005/2045 – the Income Tax (Construction Industry Scheme) Regulations 2005

These regulations were put before Parliament in July 2005, in anticipation of the new (now current) CIS to commence on 6 April 2006 – though this was deferred to 2007. There are 60 regulations with two supplementary schedules. They should be read in conjunction with sections 57 to 77 of FA 2004 (see **Appendix 3**).

The regulations lack a logical flow, and are summarised here as a quick reference.

1. Citation.

2. Interpretation of terms.

3. Multiple contractors; the sanction of one contractor with several branches, perhaps with different construction operations or in different locations, to run separate CIS registrations for each branch. This allows for delegation of duties and flexibility, rather than one centre being responsible for collating all information, or making all verifications.

4. Monthly returns; full details of the requirements and regulations.

5. Scheme representative; where a company in a group appoints another company in that group to manage its CIS requirements.

6. Verification; details of the requirements when engaging (or re-engaging if after more than two tax years) a subcontractor.

7. Payment of deductions to HMRC within 14 or 17 days.

8. Quarterly tax periods; allowed where the average monthly amount is less than £1500, stating the appropriate formula.

9. Recovery of tax not deducted; see **Chapter 14** of this book.

10. Unpaid sums; empowerment of HMRC to request a return from a contractor, or to give notice of any apparent underpayments.

11. Unpaid sums; empowerment of HMRC to issue notices to a contractor for estimated unpaid deductions and to inspect their records.

12. Certificate after inspection; empowerment of HMRC to issue a certificate to the contractor of sums liable for payment.

13. Determination; empowerment of HMRC to serve notice of a contractor's liability in the event of disputes – over the scope of CIS, or tax deductible from a subcontractor, or tax deducted but not paid.

14. Interest on amounts overdue; empowerment where applicable.

15. Interest on amounts overpaid; to be applied where applicable.

16. Recovery of amounts unpaid and interest; empowerment of HMRC to bring proceedings against a contractor.

17. In-year repayments; whereby a subcontractor can claim by the production of tax deduction statements (referred to as "vouchers"), the repayment of what is termed "provisional excess credit". This assumes that the tax for the year in which CIS deductions have been sustained can be determined at that stage. For example, a subbie with a 30 April year end could present his 2017 accounts to HMRC in say, August, and if the 2017-18 deductions already cover the tax due from those accounts (and any other income) then the excess could be reclaimed, with additional reclaims made throughout the rest of 2017-18 without having to wait until after the 2018 tax return has been submitted.

18. Small payments; this allows a contractor paying anyone else than a subbie (listed in s. 59(1)(b) to (l) – local authorities and the like) not to have to declare the payment on a monthly return if it is less than £1,000.

19. Land exemption; as 18 above, there is no need to declare a payment of less than £1,000 to someone who owns the agricultural land (as defined) on which work is undertaken.

20. Reverse premiums; this regulation excludes those from CIS, but with a caveat about capital allowances.

21. LEA agents; this excludes heads or governors of schools from having to apply CIS to anyone working on school premises.

22. Property used for business; this exempts from CIS, payments made for construction work made by a business for work on their own business property. However, excluded from this is property that is for sale, to let or held as an investment. It is not clear which has priority in the event of work on a property that is for sale but still being used in a business.

23. PFI; payments made by public bodies (s 59(1)(b) – (k)) are exempt from CIS if made under a private finance transaction.

24. Charities; payments by charities for such purposes do not fall within CIS.

25. Gross payment status; the information required by HMRC for a GPS application from a contractor, HMRC's right to refuse the application and the applicant's right of appeal against such a refusal.

26. Cancellation of GPS; confirmation of the 90 day process.

27. GPS application, business test; the identifiers to prove the contractor is in business.

28. GPS application, turnover test; the £30,000 minimum and the £200,000 (now £100,000) level for partnerships and limited companies.

29. GPS turnover test evidence; details required from established or new contractors.

30. Number of relevant persons; for partnerships or limited companies, the level is set at the maximum number of such people who held office during the qualifying period.

31. GPS turnover test; circumstances under which the principal rules are not met but can be treated as satisfactory;

32. GPS compliance test; permitted tolerances of exceptions to full compliance.

33. Absence abroad; information required to prove this, where there is no UK tax compliance record to review in the qualifying period.

34. Absence abroad; details required as proof of tax compliance in that overseas country.

35. Unemployment; details required as proof of this from either the UK authorities or from those overseas, or in the case of the latter proof of presence in that overseas country, in lieu of a tax compliance record.

36. Full-time education; details required as proof in lieu of a UK tax compliance record.

37. Interpretation of terms.

38. Interpretation of terms.

39. Electronic delivery; dependent on acceptance by the official computer system.

40. Proof of content of electronic delivery; acceptance of certification.

41. Proof of sending or receipt of electronic delivery; by the respective persons concerned unless proved to the contrary.

42. Electronic delivery on a person's behalf; not applicable if that person was not aware of its delivery or had not authorised it.

43. Proof of electronic delivery; presumed as having been done if so recorded, unless there is evidence to the contrary.

44. Proof of electronic payment; conditions as 43 above.

45. Mandatory electronic payment; linking CIS liabilities with PAYE liabilities.

46. Electronic payment by due date; definition of "received" by HMRC, the responsibility of the contractor but with the possibility of a reasonable excuse (which excludes the inability to pay).

47. Default notice; HMRC's duties and the right of appeal in the event of an apparent late payment.

48. Default surcharge; the liability of the contractor in the event of late payment(s) and a table of percentages applicable.

49. Surcharge notice and appeal; HMRC's duties and the right of appeal.

50. Delegation; HMRC officers acting on behalf of the Commissioners.

51. Inspection of records; definition of records to be produced by the contractor (hard copies and access to computer records) – or a subcontractor if they have acted as such in the last three years. Also the definition of the location of records, and HMRC's duties in the event of their removal.

52. Inspection of subcontractor records; maintenance of records as proof of deduction of tax claimed if required by an HMRC officer.

53. Close companies; for companies with GPS, the requirement to advise HMRC of a new shareholder.

54. Death of contractor; the CIS responsibility passes to the personal representatives.

55. Service by post; permission for serving notices.

56. CIS deductions and companies; the sanction, and order of offset, of CIS deductions suffered by a company against the liabilities due to HMRC arising from PAYE. In the event of an excess of deductions, the requirement for the tax year in question to have ended, and subject to HMRC being able to recover any outstanding corporation tax, before that excess can be repaid.

57. Certification of debt; the rules relating to unpaid sums.

58. Payment by cheque; treated as made on the day the cheque is received.

59. Appeals; definitions of the contractor's place of business or residence.

60. Transitional provisions; legal clarification.

Appendix 1: Construction Industry Scheme – estimated annual cost to industry

The following table provides an estimated breakdown of the annual cost to industry of operating the Construction Industry Scheme.

£m

Contractors

Regular compliance, to include:

- verification of subcontractors with HMRC and recording deduction rates;
- entering subcontractors' details into the accounting system;
- amending subcontractors' details for deduction as advised by HMRC;
- establishing whether work done falls within scope of CIS;
- checking invoices received for materials/deductible elements of charge, validating and recording;
- reviewing deductions made from weekly payments;
- reviewing deductions made from monthly payments;
- producing and issuing deduction certificates to subcontractors;
- completing monthly CIS returns and submitting online or by post,

– for 160,000 active contractors, 1.5 man hours per week @ £10 per hour   125

Cost of software:

- 75% returns filed online,

so 120,000 contractors @ £200   24

Additional accountancy costs, to include:

- verifying (and auditing where necessary) deductions made and incurred;
- providing assistance in the operation of CIS;
- applications for GPS;
- training and procedures undertaken to ensure retention of GPS;
- appealing GPS withdrawals;
- appealing incorrect CIS deductions from GPS businesses;
- reviewing business results regarding deemed contractor status;
- advising HMRC on change of control of partnerships or companies with GPS;
- employment status reviews;
- claiming and pursuing CIS repayments due to companies;
- applications for set-off of other tax liabilities against CIS repayments due;
- margins added where contractors are agencies or payrollers,

– broad, conservative estimate   35

Cost of financing excess CIS deductions:

- assuming average repayment of £3,000 across 60,000 claimants where
- excess deductions accrue evenly through the year and are repaid in July with a finance cost of 8%,

£3,000 x 9/12 x 8% x 60,000   11

Subcontractors

- Cost of collating (and requesting where necessary) deduction certificates from contractors,

– say £10 annually for 800,000 subcontractors   8

- Additional accountancy costs to verify deductions, submit tax returns and ensure repayment where applicable,

– say £25 annually for 800,000 subcontractors   20

                                                                223

Interest forgone by subcontractors

- Around £4bn is collected through CIS of which around 60% is reclaimed against SA liabilities. Assuming 800,000 subcontractors averages £3,000 each.
- If each subcontractor was paid gross and invested £250 monthly at 2% from 6 April to 5 April with payments to HMRC in January and July, this would provide £33 of interest for each year.

800,000 x £33   26

Annual cost to industry before tax relief   **249**

Appendix 2: Inland Revenue statement (1975)

Statement made in 1975 by the board of Inland Revenue about their policy on the issue, renewal and withdrawal of subcontractors' tax certificates. This statement was included in successive versions of the Revenue booklet IR40. It finally appeared in the May 2001 version but was excluded from the subsequent July 2003 version.

1. This statement explains how the Board of Inland Revenue intend to use the power, given to them under the Finance (No 2) Act 1975, to refuse Tax Certificates to businesses which have failed to comply with their taxation obligations.

2. In the first place the Board wish to dispel any fear that the threat to withhold or withdraw a certificate may be used to encourage agreement with the Inland Revenue's views in matters unrelated to the deduction Scheme. This will not happen; the question of entitlement to a certificate does not affect the taxpayer's own liability to tax and will not be brought into negotiations relating to his or her assessment – for example, where there may be a difference of opinion between the taxpayer and the Inland Revenue on a point of law or accountancy – or to the amount to be postponed pending the determination of an appeal. In such circumstances, the Inland Revenue will rely on the same legal and administrative processes in relation to the construction industry as those that apply to taxpayers generally, and will not use the threat of the refusal or withdrawal of the certificate to bypass or reinforce those procedures.

3. On the other hand, at the time when they are considering the entitlement of a business to the issue or renewal of a certificate, the Inland Revenue are bound by the Finance (No 2) Act 1975 to have regard to the extent to which there has been failure to comply with tax obligations. They intend that the powers shall be used with discretion and common sense; and minor delays in submitting accounts or returns, or other instances of non-compliance which throw no suspicion on the general tax reliability of a business, will not in themselves jeopardise entitlement to a certificate.

4. The circumstances in which the issue or renewal of a certificate will be jeopardised are where the non-compliance has been so substantial, or of such seriousness, that it gives rise to reasonable doubt about the reliability of the business in relation to the way it handles its tax affairs, and therefore to the way in which it is likely to operate the subcontractor's deduction Scheme. Apart from irregularities in connection with the deduction Scheme itself, examples of non-compliance of this order include failure to account for PAYE tax deducted, continued failure to pay the business's own tax once the amount payable has been agreed, deliberate or reckless failure to meet normal obligations (including the submitting of accounts) or to answer enquiries; or the evasion of his or her own tax liability by a person holding a key position in the business such that it gives rise to reasonable expectations that any business in which he or she holds such a position is unlikely to comply with its tax obligations. Before reaching a decision on the issue or renewal of a certificate in these cases, the Inland Revenue will, of course, take into account all the relevant factors, including the degree of involvement of the directors or proprietors as a whole and any extenuating circumstances.

5. Once issued, a certificate will be withdrawn during its period of validity only if there has been serious irregularity in the operation of the subcontractor's deduction Scheme, or in the case of some significant occurrence (such as a change in the persons controlling the business) which gives reason to doubt whether there will continue to be compliance with the Scheme. In such cases, it would be usual for the certificate holder to receive some form of preliminary warning. There may, however, be exceptional cases where immediate action, without warning, to withdraw the certificate will be the only way in which the Inland Revenue can be protected.

Appendix 3: FA 2004 – key legislation

This appendix reproduces FA 2004, sections 57 to 77, as amended.

57   Introduction

(1)   This Chapter provides for certain payments (see section 60) under construction contracts to be made under deduction of sums on account of tax (see sections 61 and 62).

(2)   In this Chapter "construction contract" means a contract relating to construction operations (see section 74) which is not a contract of employment but where–

    (a)   one party to the contract is a sub-contractor (see section 58); and

    (b)   another party to the contract ("the contractor") either–

        (i)   is a sub-contractor under another such contract relating to all or any of the construction operations, or

        (ii)   is a person to whom section 59 applies.

(3)   In sections 60 and 61 "the contractor" has the meaning given by this section.

(4)   In this Chapter–

    (a)   references to registration for gross payment are to registration under section 63(2),

    (b)   references to registration for payment under deduction are to registration under section 63(3), and

    (c)   references to registration under section 63 are to registration for gross payment or registration for payment under deduction.

(5)   To the extent that any provision of this Chapter would not, apart from this subsection, form part of the Tax Acts, it shall be taken to form part of those Acts.

58   Sub-contractors

For the purposes of this Chapter a party to a contract relating to construction operations is a sub-contractor if, under the contract–

(a)   he is under a duty to the contractor to carry out the operations, or to furnish his own labour (in the case of a company, the labour of employees or officers of the company) or the labour of others in the carrying out of the operations or to arrange for the labour of others to be furnished in the carrying out of the operations; or

(b)   he is answerable to the contractor for the carrying out of the operations by others, whether under a contract or under other arrangements made or to be made by him.

59   Contractors

(1)   This section applies to the following bodies or persons–

(a)   any person carrying on a business which includes construction operations;

(b)   any public office or department of the Crown (including any Northern Ireland department, the Welsh Assembly Government and any part of the Scottish Administration);

(c)   the Corporate Officer of the House of Lords, the Corporate Officer of the House of Commons, the Scottish Parliamentary Corporate Body and the National Assembly for Wales Commission;

(d)   any local authority;

(e)   any development corporation or new town commission;

(f)   the Homes and Communities Agency;

(fa)   the Greater London Authority in the exercise of its functions relating to housing or regeneration or its new towns and urban development functions;

(g)   the Secretary of State if the contract is made by him under section 89 of the Housing Associations Act 1985 (c. 69);

(h)   the Regulator of Social Housing, a housing association, a housing trust, Scottish Homes, and the Northern Ireland Housing Executive;

(i)   any NHS trust;

(j)   any HSS trust;

(k)   any such body or person, being a body or person (in addition to those falling within paragraphs (b) to (j)) which has been established for the purpose of carrying out functions conferred on it by or under any enactment, as may be designated as a body or person to which this section applies in regulations made by the Board of Inland Revenue;

(l)   a person carrying on a business at any time if–

    (i)   his average annual expenditure on construction operations in the period of three years ending with the end of the last period of account before that time exceeds £1,000,000, or

    (ii)   where he was not carrying on the business at the beginning of that period of three years, one-third of his total expenditure on construction operations for the part of that period during which he has been carrying on the business exceeds £1,000,000.

(2)   But this section only applies to a body or person falling within subsection (1)(b) to (fa) or (h) to (k) if–

    (a)   in any period of three years, that body or person has had an average annual expenditure on construction operations of more than £1,000,000, and

    (b)   since the condition in paragraph (a) was last satisfied, there have not been three successive years in each of which the body or person has had expenditure on construction operations of less than £1,000,000.

In this subsection "year" means a year ending with 31st March.

(3)   Where section 57(2)(b) begins to apply to a person in any period of account by virtue of his falling within subsection (1)(l), it shall continue to apply to him until he satisfies the Board of Inland Revenue that his expenditure on construction operations has been less than £1,000,000 in each of three successive years beginning in or after that period of account.

(4)   Where the whole or part of a trade is transferred by a company ("the transferor") to another company ("the transferee") and Chapter 1 of Part 22 of the Corporation Tax Act 2010 has effect in relation to the transfer, then in determining for the purposes of this section the amount of expenditure incurred by the transferee–

   (a)   the whole or, as the case may be, a proportionate part of any expenditure incurred by the transferor at a time before the transfer is to be treated as if it had been incurred at that time by the transferee; and

   (b)   where only a part of the trade is transferred, the expenditure is to be apportioned in such manner as appears to the Board of Inland Revenue, or on appeal to the tribunal, to be just and reasonable.

(5)   In this section–

   • "development corporation" has the same meaning as in–

      (a)   the New Towns Act 1981 (c. 64), or
      (b)   the New Towns (Scotland) Act 1968 (c. 16);

   • "enactment" includes an enactment comprised in an Act of the Scottish Parliament and a provision comprised in Northern Ireland legislation;
   • "housing association" has the same meaning as in–

      (a)   the Housing Associations Act 1985 (c. 69), or
      (b)   Part 2 of the Housing (Northern Ireland) Order 1992 (S.I. 1992/ 1725 (N.I. 15));

   • "housing trust" has the same meaning as in the Housing Associations Act 1985;

- "HSS trust" means a Health and Social Services trust established under the Health and Personal Social Services (Northern Ireland) Order 1991 (S.I. 1991/194 (N.I. 1));
- "new town commission" has the same meaning as in the New Towns Act (Northern Ireland) 1965 (c. 13 (N.I.));
- "NHS trust" means a National Health Service trust–

    (a)   established under section 25 of the National Health Service Act 2006 or section 18 of the National Health Service (Wales) Act 2006, or

    (b)   constituted under section 12A of the National Health Service (Scotland) Act 1978 (c. 29).

(6)   In this section references to a body or person include references to an office or department.

(7)   The Board of Inland Revenue may make regulations amending this section for the purpose of removing references to bodies which have ceased to exist.

(8)   This section is subject to section 73A (designated international organisations: exemption from section 59).

Deductions on account of tax from contract payments to sub-contractors

60   Contract payments

(1)   In this Chapter "contract payment" means any payment which is made under a construction contract and is so made by the contractor (see section 57(3)) to–

    (a)   the sub-contractor,

    (b)   a person nominated by the sub-contractor or the contractor, or

    (c)   a person nominated by a person who is a sub-contractor under another such contract relating to all or any of the construction operations.

(2)   But a payment made under a construction contract is not a contract payment if any of the following exceptions applies in relation to it.

(3)   This exception applies if the payment is treated as earnings from an employment by virtue of Chapter 7 of Part 2 of the Income Tax (Earnings and Pensions) Act 2003 (c. 1) (agency workers).

(4)   This exception applies if the person to whom the payment is made or, in the case of a payment made to a nominee, each of the following persons–

(a)   the nominee,

(b)   the person who nominated him, and

(c)   the person for whose labour (or, where that person is a company, for whose employees' or officers' labour) the payment is made,

is registered for gross payment when the payment is made.

But this is subject to subsections (5) and (6).

(5)   Where a person is registered for gross payment as a partner in a firm (see section 64), subsection (4) applies only in relation to payments made under contracts under which–

(a)   the firm is a sub-contractor, or

(b)   where a person has nominated the firm to receive payments, the person who has nominated the firm is a sub-contractor.

(6)   Where a person is registered for gross payment otherwise than as a partner in a firm but he is or becomes a partner in a firm, subsection (4) does not apply in relation to payments made under contracts under which–

(a)   the firm is a sub-contractor, or

(b)   where a person has nominated the firm to receive payments, the person who has nominated the firm is a sub-contractor.

(7) This exception applies if such conditions as may be prescribed in regulations made by the Board of Inland Revenue for the purposes of this subsection are satisfied; and those conditions may relate to any one or more of the following–

   (a) the payment,

   (b) the person making it, and

   (c) the person receiving it.

(8) For the purposes of this Chapter a payment (including a payment by way of loan) that has the effect of discharging an obligation under a contract relating to construction operations is to be taken to be made under the contract; and if–

   (a) the obligation is to make a payment to a person ("A") within paragraph (a) to (c) of subsection (1), but

   (b) the payment discharging that obligation is made to a person ("B") not within those paragraphs,

   the payment is for those purposes to be taken to be made to A.

61 Deductions on account of tax from contract payments

(1) On making a contract payment the contractor (see section 57(3)) must deduct from it a sum equal to the relevant percentage of so much of the payment as is not shown to represent the direct cost to any other person of materials used or to be used in carrying out the construction operations to which the contract under which the payment is to be made relates.

(2) In subsection (1) "the relevant percentage" means such percentage as the Treasury may by order determine.

(3) That percentage must not exceed–

   (a) if the person for whose labour (or for whose employees' or officers' labour) the payment in question is made is registered for payment under deduction, the percentage which is the basic rate for the year of assessment in which the payment is made, or

(b)　if that person is not so registered, the percentage which is the higher rate for that year of assessment.

62　Treatment of sums deducted

(1)　A sum deducted under section 61 from a payment made by a contractor–

(a)　must be paid to the Board of Inland Revenue, and

(b)　is to be treated for the purposes of income tax or, as the case may be, corporation tax as not diminishing the amount of the payment.

(2)　If the sub-contractor is not a company a sum deducted under section 61 and paid to the Board is to be treated as being income tax paid in respect of the sub-contractor's relevant profits.

If the sum is more than sufficient to discharge his liability to income tax in respect of those profits, so much of the excess as is required to discharge any liability of his for Class 4 contributions is to be treated as being Class 4 contributions paid in respect of those profits.

(3)　If the sub-contractor is a company–

(a)　a sum deducted under section 61 and paid to the Board is to be treated, in accordance with regulations, as paid on account of any relevant liabilities of the sub-contractor;

(b)　regulations must provide for the sum to be applied in discharging relevant liabilities of the year of assessment in which the deduction is made;

(c)　if the amount is more than sufficient to discharge the sub-contractor's relevant liabilities, the excess may be treated, in accordance with the regulations, as being corporation tax paid in respect of the sub-contractor's relevant profits; and

(d) regulations must provide for the repayment to the sub-contractor of any amount not required for the purposes mentioned in paragraphs (b) and (c).

(4) For the purposes of subsection (3) the "relevant liabilities" of a sub-contractor are any liabilities of the sub-contractor, whether arising before or after the deduction is made, to make a payment to the Inland Revenue in pursuance of an obligation as an employer or contractor.

(5) In this section–

(a) "the sub-contractor" means the person for whose labour (or for whose employees' or officers' labour) the payment is made;

(b) references to the sub-contractor's "relevant profits" are to the profits from the trade, profession or vocation carried on by him in the course of which the payment was received;

(c) "Class 4 contributions" means Class 4 contributions within the meaning of the Social Security Contributions and Benefits Act 1992 (c. 4) or the Social Security Contributions and Benefits (Northern Ireland) Act 1992 (c. 7).

(6) References in this section to regulations are to regulations made by the Board of Inland Revenue.

(7) Regulations under this section may contain such supplementary, incidental or consequential provision as appears to the Board to be appropriate.

Registration of sub-contractors

63 Registration for gross payment or for payment under deduction

(1) If the Board of Inland Revenue are satisfied, on the application of an individual or a company, that the applicant has provided–

(a)   such documents, records and information as may be required by or in accordance with regulations made by the Board, and

(b)   such additional documents, records and information as may be required by the Inland Revenue in connection with the application,

the Board must register the individual or company under this section.

(2)   If the Board are satisfied that the requirements of subsection (2), (3) or (4) of section 64 are met, the Board must register–

(a)   the individual or company, or

(b)   in a case falling within subsection (3) of that section, the individual or company as a partner in the firm in question,

for gross payment.

(3)   In any other case, the Board must register the individual or company for payment under deduction.

64   Requirements for registration for gross payment

(1)   This section sets out the requirements (in addition to that in subsection (1) of section 63) for an applicant to be registered for gross payment.

(2)   Where the application is for the registration for gross payment of an individual (otherwise than as a partner in a firm), he must satisfy the conditions in Part 1 of Schedule 11 to this Act.

(3)   Where the application is for the registration for gross payment of an individual or a company as a partner in a firm–

(a)   the applicant must satisfy the conditions in Part 1 of Schedule 11 to this Act (if an individual) or Part 3 of that Schedule (if a company), and

(b)   in either case, the firm itself must satisfy the conditions in Part 2 of that Schedule.

(4) Where the application is for the registration for gross payment of a company (otherwise than as a partner in a firm)–

    (a) the company must satisfy the conditions in Part 3 of Schedule 11 to this Act, and

    (b) if the Board of Inland Revenue have given a direction under subsection (5), each of the persons to whom any of the conditions in Part 1 of that Schedule applies in accordance with the direction must satisfy the conditions which so apply to him.

(5) Where the applicant is a company, the Board may direct that the conditions in Part 1 of Schedule 11 to this Act or such of them as are specified in the direction shall apply to–

    (a) the directors of the company,

    (b) if the company is a close company, the persons who are the beneficial owners of shares in the company, or

    (c) such of those directors or persons as are so specified,

as if each of them were an applicant for registration for gross payment.

(6) See also section 65(1) (power of Board to make direction under subsection (5) on change in control of company applying for registration etc).

(7) In subsection (5) "director" has the meaning given by section 67 of the Income Tax (Earnings and Pensions) Act 2003 (c. 1).

65 Change in control of company registered for gross payment

(1) Where it appears to the Board of Inland Revenue that there has been a change in the control of a company–

    (a) registered for gross payment, or

    (b) applying to be so registered,

the Board may make a direction under section 64(5).

(2) The Board may make regulations requiring the furnishing of information with respect to changes in the control of a company–

(a) registered for gross payment, or

(b) applying to be so registered.

(3) In this section references to a change in the control of a company are references to such a change determined in accordance with section 995 of the Income Tax Act 2007.

66   Cancellation of registration for gross payment

(1) The Board of Inland Revenue may at any time make a determination cancelling a person's registration for gross payment if it appears to them that–

(a) if an application to register the person for gross payment were to be made at that time, the Board would refuse so to register him,

(b) he has made an incorrect return or provided incorrect information (whether as a contractor or as a sub-contractor) under any provision of this Chapter or of regulations made under it, or

(c) he has failed to comply (whether as a contractor or as a sub-contractor) with any such provision.

(2) Where the Board make a determination under subsection (1), the person's registration for gross payment is cancelled with effect from the end of a prescribed period after the making of the determination (but see section 67(5)).

(3) The Board of Inland Revenue may at any time make a determination cancelling a person's registration for gross payment if they have reasonable grounds to suspect that the person–

(a) became registered for gross payment on the basis of information which was false,

(b) has fraudulently made an incorrect return or provided incorrect information (whether as a contractor or as a sub-contractor) under any provision of this Chapter or of regulations made under it, or

(c)   has knowingly failed to comply (whether as a contractor or as a sub-contractor) with any such provision.

(4)   Where the Board make a determination under subsection (3), the person's registration for gross payment is cancelled with immediate effect.

(5)   On making a determination under this section cancelling a person's registration for gross payment, the Board must without delay give the person notice stating the reasons for the cancellation.

(6)   Where a person's registration for gross payment is cancelled by virtue of a determination under subsection (1), the person must be registered for payment under deduction.

(7)   Where a person's registration for gross payment is cancelled by virtue of a determination under subsection (3), the person may, if the Board thinks fit, be registered for payment under deduction.

(8)   A person whose registration for gross payment is cancelled under this section may not, within the period of one year after the cancellation takes effect (see subsections (2) and (4) and section 67(5)), apply for registration for gross payment.

(9)   In this section "a prescribed period" means a period prescribed by regulations made by the Board.

67   Registration for gross payment: appeals

(1)   A person aggrieved by–

(a)   the refusal of an application for registration for gross payment, or

(b)   the cancellation of his registration for gross payment,

may by notice appeal.

(2) The notice must be given to the Board of Inland Revenue within 30 days after the refusal or cancellation.

(3) The notice must state the person's reasons for believing that–

    (a) the application should not have been refused, or

    (b) his registration for gross payment should not have been cancelled.

(4) The jurisdiction of the tribunal on such an appeal that is notified to the tribunal shall include jurisdiction to review any relevant decision taken by the Board of Inland Revenue in the exercise of their functions under section 63, 64, 65 or 66.

(5) Where a person appeals against the cancellation of his registration for gross payment by virtue of a determination under section 66(1), the cancellation of his registration does not take effect until whichever is the latest of the following–

    (a) the abandonment of the appeal,

    (b) the determination of the appeal by the tribunal, or

    (c) the determination of the appeal by the Upper Tribunal or a court.

68 Registration for payment under deduction: cancellation and appeals

The Board of Inland Revenue may make regulations providing for–

    (a) the cancellation, in such circumstances as may be prescribed by the regulations, of a person's registration for payment under deduction;

    (b) appeals against a refusal to register a person for payment under deduction or the cancellation of such registration.

Verification, returns etc and penalties

69 Verification etc of registration status of sub-contractors

(1) The Board of Inland Revenue may make regulations requiring persons who make payments under contracts

relating to construction operations, except in prescribed circumstances, to verify with the Board whether a person to whom they are proposing to make–

(a)   a contract payment, or

(b)   a payment which would be a contract payment but for section 60(4),

is registered for gross payment or for payment under deduction.

(2)   The provision that may be made by regulations under subsection (1) includes provision–

(a)   for preventing a person from verifying unless such conditions as may be prescribed have been satisfied;

(b)   as to the period for which the verification remains valid.

(3)   The Board of Inland Revenue may make regulations requiring the Board to notify persons of a prescribed description who make payments under contracts relating to construction operations that–

(a)   a person registered for gross payment has become registered for payment under deduction or has ceased to be registered under section 63, or

(b)   a person registered for payment under deduction has become registered for gross payment or has ceased to be registered under section 63.

(4)   The provision that may be made by regulations under subsection (1) or (3) includes provision for a person to be entitled to assume, except in prescribed circumstances, that–

(a)   a person verified or notified as being registered for gross payment, or

(b)   a person verified or notified as being registered for payment under deduction,

has not subsequently ceased to be so registered.

(5)   In this section "prescribed" means prescribed by regulations under this section.

70   Periodic returns by contractors etc

(1)   The Board of Inland Revenue may make regulations requiring persons who make payments under construction contracts–

    (a)   to make to the Board, at such times and in respect of such periods as may be prescribed, returns relating to such payments;

    (b)   to keep such records as may be prescribed relating to such payments;

    (c)   to provide such information as may be prescribed, at such times as may be prescribed, to persons to whom such payments are made or to such of those persons as are of a prescribed description.

(2)   The provision that may be made by regulations under subsection (1)(a) includes provision requiring, except in such circumstances as may be prescribed,–

    (a)   the person making a return to declare in the return that none of the contracts to which the return relates is a contract of employment;

    (b)   the person making a return to declare in the return that, in the case of each person to whom a payment to which the return relates is made, he has complied with the requirements of any regulations made under section 69(1) (verification of registration status);

    (c)   returns to contain such other information and to be in such form as may be prescribed;

    (d)   a return to be made where no payments have been made in the period to which the return relates.

(3)   The Board of Inland Revenue may make regulations with respect to–

    (a)   the production, copying and removal of, and the making of extracts from, any records kept by virtue of any such requirement as is referred to in subsection (1)(b), and

(b) rights of access to, or copies of, any such records which are removed.

(4) Regulations under this section may make provision–

(a) for or in connection with enabling a person who makes payments under construction contracts to appoint another person (a "scheme representative") to act on his behalf in connection with any requirements imposed on him by regulations under this section, and

(b) as to the rights, obligations or liabilities of scheme representatives.

(5) In this section "prescribed" means prescribed by regulations under this section.

71 Collection and recovery of sums to be deducted

(1) The Board of Inland Revenue must make regulations with respect to the collection and recovery, whether by assessment or otherwise, of sums required to be deducted from any payments under section 61.

(2) The regulations may include any matters with respect to which PAYE regulations may be made.

(3) Interest required to be paid by the regulations–

(a) is to be paid without any deduction of income tax, and

(b) [repealed by CTA 2009, s. 1326 and Sch. 3, Pt. 1].

72 Penalties

If a person, for the purpose of becoming registered for gross payment or for payment under deduction,–

(a) makes any statement, or furnishes any document, which he knows to be false in a material particular, or

(b) recklessly makes any statement, or furnishes any document, which is false in a material particular,

he shall be liable to a penalty not exceeding £3,000.

Supplementary

73 Regulations under this Chapter: supplementary

(1) The Board of Inland Revenue may by regulations make such other provision for giving effect to this Chapter as they consider necessary or expedient.

(2) The provision that may be made by regulations under subsection (1) includes provision for or in connection with modifying the application of this Chapter in circumstances where–

    (a) a person acts as the agent of a contractor or sub-contractor;

    (b) a person's right to payments under a construction contract is assigned or otherwise transferred to another person.

(3) Regulations under this Chapter may make different provision for different cases.

(4) Any power under this Chapter to make regulations authorising or requiring a document (whether or not of a particular description), or any records or information, to be given or requested by or to be sent or produced to the Board of Inland Revenue includes power–

    (a) to authorise the Board to nominate a person who is not an officer of the Board to be the person who on behalf of the Board–

        (i) gives or requests the document, records or information; or

        (ii) is the recipient of the document, records or information; and

    (b) to require the document, records or information, in cases prescribed by or determined under the regulations, to be sent or produced to the address (determined in accordance with the regulations) of the person nominated by the Board to receive it on their behalf.

73A Designated international organisations: exemption from section 59

(1) The Treasury may by order designate for the purposes of this section any international organisation of which the United Kingdom is a member.

(2) Section 59 does not apply to an organisation which is so designated.

74 Meaning of "construction operations"

(1) In this Chapter "construction operations" means operations of a description specified in subsection (2), not being operations of a description specified in subsection (3); and references to construction operations–

    (a) except where the context otherwise requires, include references to the work of individuals participating in the carrying out of such operations; and

    (b) do not include references to operations carried out or to be carried out otherwise than in the United Kingdom (or the territorial sea of the United Kingdom).

(2) The following operations are, subject to subsection (3), construction operations for the purposes of this Chapter–

    (a) construction, alteration, repair, extension, demolition or dismantling of buildings or structures (whether permanent or not), including offshore installations;

    (b) construction, alteration, repair, extension or demolition of any works forming, or to form, part of the land, including (in particular) walls, roadworks, power-lines, electronic communications apparatus, aircraft runways, docks and harbours, railways, inland waterways, pipe-lines, reservoirs, water-mains, wells, sewers, industrial plant and installations for purposes of land drainage, coast protection or defence;

(c)   installation in any building or structure of systems of heating, lighting, air-conditioning, ventilation, power supply, drainage, sanitation, water supply or fire protection;

(d)   internal cleaning of buildings and structures, so far as carried out in the course of their construction, alteration, repair, extension or restoration;

(e)   painting or decorating the internal or external surfaces of any building or structure;

(f)   operations which form an integral part of, or are preparatory to, or are for rendering complete, such operations as are previously described in this subsection, including site clearance, earth-moving, excavation, tunnelling and boring, laying of foundations, erection of scaffolding, site restoration, landscaping and the provision of roadways and other access works.

(3)   The following operations are not construction operations for the purposes of this Chapter–

(a)   drilling for, or extraction of, oil or natural gas;

(b)   extraction (whether by underground or surface working) of minerals and tunnelling or boring, or construction of underground works, for this purpose;

(c)   manufacture of building or engineering components or equipment, materials, plant or machinery, or delivery of any of these things to site;

(d)   manufacture of components for systems of heating, lighting, air-conditioning, ventilation, power supply, drainage, sanitation, water supply or fire protection, or delivery of any of these things to site;

(e)   the professional work of architects or surveyors, or of consultants in building, engineering, interior or exterior decoration or in the laying-out of landscape;

(f) the making, installation and repair of artistic works, being sculptures, murals and other works which are wholly artistic in nature;

(g) signwriting and erecting, installing and repairing signboards and advertisements;

(h) the installation of seating, blinds and shutters;

(i) the installation of security systems, including burglar alarms, closed circuit television and public address systems.

(4) The Treasury may by order made by statutory instrument amend either or both of subsections (2) and (3) by–

(a) adding,

(b) varying, or

(c) removing,

any description of operations.

(5) No statutory instrument containing an order under subsection (4) shall be made unless a draft of the instrument has been laid before and approved by a resolution of the House of Commons.

75 Meaning of "the Inland Revenue" etc and delegation of Board's functions

(1) In this Chapter "the Inland Revenue" means any officer of the Board of Inland Revenue.

(2) In this Chapter "the Board of Inland Revenue" means the Commissioners of Inland Revenue (as to which, see in particular the Inland Revenue Regulation Act 1890 (c. 21)).

(3) The Board of Inland Revenue may make regulations providing for any of the following to be done on behalf of the Board–

(a) the registration of persons under section 63;

(b) the giving of directions under section 64(5); and

(c) the cancellation under section 66 of a person's registration for gross payment.

76 Consequential amendments

Schedule 12 to this Act (which makes consequential amendments) has effect.

77 Commencement and transitional provision

(1) This Chapter has effect in relation to payments made on or after the appointed day under contracts relating to construction operations.

(2) Where a certificate issued to a person under section 561 of the Taxes Act 1988 is in force immediately before the appointed day, the person is to be treated as if, on the appointed day, the Board of Inland Revenue had registered him for gross payment.

(3) Where a registration card issued to a person in accordance with regulations made under section 566(2A) of the Taxes Act 1988 is in force immediately before the appointed day, the person is to be treated as if, on the appointed day, the Board of Inland Revenue had registered him for payment under deduction.

(4) Subsection (5) applies in relation to the first payment ("the relevant payment") made after the appointed day by a person ("C") to a sub-contractor ("SC") under a contract relating to construction operations if–

    (a) before the appointed day, C had made one or more payments to SC under the contract or another such contract,

    (b) the last of those payments ("the last payment") was made in the year of assessment in which the relevant payment was made or in either of the two years of assessment before that,

    (c) at the time of the last payment–

        (i) a certificate issued to SC under section 561 of the Taxes Act 1988 was in force, or

        (ii) a registration card issued to SC in accordance with regulations made under section 566(2A) of that Act was in force, and

      (d)   on making the relevant payment, C has no reason to believe that SC–

          (i)   did not become registered for gross payment or (as the case may be) for payment under deduction by virtue of subsection (2) or (3), and

          (ii)   is not still so registered.

(5)   Where this subsection applies, regulations under section 69(1) shall not require C, before making the relevant payment, to verify whether SC is registered for gross payment or for payment under deduction.

(6)   Where subsection (5) applies, C shall be entitled to assume, on making any further payments to SC under a contract relating to construction operations, that SC has not subsequently ceased to be so registered, unless notified to the contrary in accordance with regulations made under section 69(3).

(7)   In this section "the appointed day" means such day as the Treasury may by order appoint.

(8)   The Treasury may by order make such further supplemental and transitional provision and savings as they think fit in connection with the coming into effect of this Chapter.

Appendix 4: Local authorities and other public bodies

This appendix reproduces paragraph CISR 13040 from the Construction Industry Scheme Reform Manual.

The Scheme: subcontractors: local authorities and other public bodies as subcontractors

Local Authorities and many public bodies are deemed to be contractors where they spend over a certain amount on construction operations (See CISR12050 for more about 'deemed contractors').

Local Authorities and the following public bodies are also subcontractors when carrying out construction operations. Although they will not be formally registered on CIS, they are to be regarded as holding gross payment status. The deduction scheme should not be applied, and no deductions should be made from payments to them.

- Port of London Authority
- Port of Tyne Authority
- Commission for the New Towns
- UK Atomic Energy Authority
- Welsh Development Agency
- Scottish Enterprise
- Registered Housing Associations and Societies
- British Broadcasting Corporation
- Government Departments and Executive Agencies
- Environment Agency
- British Waterways Board (up to 2 July 2012)
- Scottish Canals
- Transport for London
- Health Service bodies and NHS Trusts
- Olympic Development Authority (ODA)
- London Legacy Development Corporation (LLDC)

Where a local authority sets up a Direct Labour Organisation (DLO) or Direct Service Organisation (DSO) to carry out construction operations, and the organisation remains part of the local authority, it is covered by the exemption described above which applies to local authorities. It may be treated as holding gross payment status. Where, however, a DLO or DSO incorporates it becomes a separate company liable to Corporation Tax even if wholly controlled by the local authority. Such a company must apply for registration to be paid gross or net to receive payments falling within the scope of the Scheme.

If a public body or utility is privatised, it is then just like any other private business and must be registered on CIS to enable it to receive payments under the Scheme.

Table of legislation

Taxes Management Act 1970

Index of cases

General index

Printed and bound in Great Britain by
Marston Book Services Limited, Oxfordshire